ECDL

Advanced Presentation

ECDL
Advanced Presentation

**Sadhbh O'Dwyer
and Paul Holden**

Approved
Courseware
Advanced
Syllabus AM 6
Version 1.0

PEARSON
Prentice
Hall

Harlow, England • London • New York • Boston • San Francisco • Toronto • Sydney • Singapore • Hong Kong
Tokyo • Seoul • Taipei • New Delhi • Cape Town • Madrid • Mexico City • Amsterdam • Munich • Paris • Milan

PEARSON EDUCATION LIMITED

Edinburgh Gate
Harlow
Essex CM20 2JE
England

and Associated Companies throughout the world

Visit us on the World Wide Web at:
www.pearsoned.co.uk

First published in 2004

The screenshots in this book are reprinted by permission from Microsoft Corporation.

'European Computer Driving Licence' and ECDL and Stars device are registered trademarks of The European Computer Driving Licence Foundation Limited in Ireland and other countries. Pearson Education Ltd is an independent entity from The European Computer Driving Licence Foundation Limited, and not affiliated with The European Computer Driving Licence Foundation Limited in any manner. *ECDL Advanced Presentation* may be used in assisting students to prepare for the ECDL AM6 tests. Neither The European Computer Driving Licence Foundation Limited nor Pearson Education Ltd warrants that the use of this coursebook will ensure passing the ECDL AM6 tests. Use of the ECDL-F Approved Courseware Logo on this product signifies that it has been independently reviewed and approved by ECDL-F as complying with the following standards:

Acceptable coverage of all courseware content related to the ECDL AM6 Syllabus Version 1.0

This courseware material does not guarantee that the end user will pass the ECDL AM6 tests. Any and all assessment items and/or performance based exercises contained in this coursebook relate solely to this product and do not constitute or imply certification by The European Driving Licence Foundation in respect of any ECDL examination. For details on sitting ECDL examinations in your country please contact your country's National ECDL/ICDL designated Licensee or visit The European Computer Driving Licence Foundation Limited web site at http://www.ecdl.com.

Candidates using this courseware material should have a valid ECDL/ICDL Skills Card. Without such a Skills Card, no ECDL/ICDL Examinations can be taken and no ECDL/ICDL certificate, nor any other form of recognition, can be given to the candidate.

ECDL/ICDL Skills Cards may be obtained from any Approved ECDL/ICDL Test Centre or from your country's National ECDL/ICDL designated Licensee.

References to the European Computer Driving Licence (ECDL) include the International Computer Driving Licence (ICDL). AM6 is published as the official syllabus for use within the European Computer Driving Licence (ECDL) and International Computer Driving Licence (ICDL) certification programme.

ISBN 0131202413

British Library Cataloguing-in-Publication Data
A catalogue record for this book is available from the British Library

10 9 8 7 6 5 4 3 2 1
08 07 06 05 04

Typeset in 11pt TimesNewRomanPS by 30.
Printed and bound by Ashford Colour Press, in Gosport.

The Publishers' policy is to use paper manufactured from sustainable forests.

Contents

Chapter 4: Flowcharts   38

Chapter 5: Charts   57

Chapter 6: Action buttons and hyperlinks 72

Chapter 7: Custom shows and slide shows 87

Chapter 8: Transitions 98

Chapter 11: Linking   146

Chapter 12: Macros and set-ups   160

Preface

What is ECDL?

ECDL, or the European Computer Driving Licence, is an internationally recognised qualification in Information Technology skills. It is accepted by businesses internationally as a verification of competence and proficiency in computer skills.

The ECDL syllabus is neither operating system nor software specific.

For more information about ECDL, and to see the syllabus for *ECDL Module 6, Presentation, Advanced Level*, visit the official ECDL website at http://www.ecdl.com.

About this book

This book covers the ECDL Advanced Presentation Syllabus Version 1.0, using PowerPoint 2000 to complete all the required tasks. It is assumed that you have already completed the presentation module of ECDL 4.0 or earlier, using PowerPoint, or have an equivalent knowledge of the product.

Each chapter in this book contains a number of exercises. You can work through these exercises either sequentially or in any order you choose. Each exercise incorporates the results of preceding exercises. The starting points for the exercises are available on the CD that accompanies this book. If you are working though the book sequentially, you may wish to save your finished exercises in a different folder to the exercises supplied on CD.

Additional exercises, labelled Quick Quiz, have been posed for you to complete. These exercises provide limited guidance as to how to go about performing the tasks, since you should have learned what you need in the preceding exercises.

Hardware and software requirements

- CD-ROM drive

- 500 KB of free space on your hard disk

- PowerPoint 2000, PowerPoint 97 or PowerPoint XP

- Word 2000, Word 97 or Word XP

Note: The examples and exercises in this book are based on Microsoft Office 2000. If you are using a different version of Office, some of the screens and operations may be slightly different, but the general principles still apply.

Typographic conventions

The following typographic conventions are used in this book:

Bold face text is used to denote command names, button names, menu names, the names of tabs in dialog boxes, and keyboard keys.

Italicized text is used to denote options in drop-down lists and list boxes, dialog box names, areas in dialog boxes and toolbars.

CAPITALIZED TEXT is used to denote file types and exercise files.

1

Getting started

The case study

The exercises in this book relate to the presentations used by the fictitious company, Green Grocer Group, or GGG.

The Green Grocer Group is an organic food supplier. They supply major retailers with high quality organic fruit and vegetables. GGG source their produce from organic farmers in several locations. All produce of the Green Grocer Group is certified organic and is traceable. Due to the high demand for organic produce, GGG is expanding and is looking for new stockists and suppliers.

Your brief is to create an overview presentation that is of relevance to both the farmers who supply GGG with organic produce and the investors in the company.

The CD

The CD supplied with this book contains exercise files and the following supplementary files:

- GGG.DOC – Word outline of the presentation
- PREVIOUS.PPT – Previous PowerPoint presentation from the Green Grocer Group
- GGG.JPG – Green Grocer Group logo
- ORGANICS.JPG – Organic Farming in Europe logo
- FIELD.WMV – Organic farm video
- BOWL1.JPG – Fruit bowl graphic
- GREEN GROCER GROUP.MDB – Database of best-selling goods
- SUPPLIERS.XLS – Spreadsheet of suppliers
- WHAT OUR CUSTOMERS SAY.DOC – Word document
- END OF YEAR RESULTS.XLS – Spreadsheet of financial results

You will use these files when completing the exercises in the book.

Copying files from the CD

Before you begin working through the exercises in this book, you will need to copy the files from the CD to your computer. Create a folder on your computer and copy the files from the CD to it. Ideally, you should also create a subfolder within this folder into which you can save your completed exercises.

Exercise 1.1: Copying files from the CD to your computer

1) Create a folder called ECDL_PRESENTATIONS anywhere on your computer. This will be your working folder for the exercises in this book.

2) Copy all the files from the CD to the ECDL_PRESENTATIONS folder.

3) Create a sub-folder within the ECDL_PRESENTATIONS folder for completed exercises. Name this folder EXERCISE_COMPLETE. You can save your completed exercises into here.

Information structure

To communicate your message successfully you need to structure your information and present it clearly.

PowerPoint enables you to do both these things. In this chapter you will focus on structuring information in your PowerPoint presentation so that it is clear and easy to follow. You will gain an appreciation for the role of the audience in your presentation, and learn how to build your presentation around their needs.

New skills

At the end of this chapter you should be able to:

- Plan a presentation
- Build your presentation around the needs of the audience
- Organize your information into accessible units
- Import a Word document into a presentation

New words

At the end of this chapter you should be able to explain the following term:

- 7±2 rule

Syllabus reference

This chapter covers the following syllabus points:

- AM 6.1.1.1
- AM 6.1.1.2
- AM 6.1.3.1
- AM 6.2.1.2
- AM 6.2.1.3

Planning

A good presentation starts with a clear plan. A plan takes into account the following:

- Who am I talking to?
- What am I trying to say?
- How long will my presentation take?
- What hardware will I be using?
- Where will my presentation take place?

Don't open your presentation software yet; first you've got to think about your audience.

The audience

Think about it: you are giving this presentation so that your audience will be informed, convinced, entertained, influenced or educated. A good presentation, therefore, is planned around your audience, their needs and your message.

The more you know about the demographic profile of your audience, the better you can tailor your presentation to their needs. Ask questions such as – What are these people like? How old are they? Where do they live? What do they do? What is their level of education? What do they like? What do they dislike?

The answers to these questions help you to choose appropriate language and level of detail, tone, suitable examples, imagery and so on.

As the audience for the case study in this book consists of two distinct groups – suppliers of organic food, and shareholders in the organic food company, Green Grocer Group – your message should satisfy the needs of both. The suppliers will want to know about the growth of their produce and the shareholders will want to know about the growth of their shares!

Use of language

This audience is a mixture of the business community and the agricultural community. Some of the shareholders might need explanations of the agricultural terms; some of the suppliers might need explanations of the business terms. Accordingly, you may need to explain some terms that are specific to each group.

Keep your language consistent. Use the same terms to describe the same things, otherwise your audience might get confused. If you use jargon or technical terms, be sure that your audience understands them.

Cultural differences

An audience may misinterpret the message of a presentation due to cultural differences between them and the presenter. If you are presenting to a group from a different country, for example, you should be sensitive to possible misinterpretations. Some cultures, for example, read from right to left; if your slides depend on a left-right flow, such an audience might not be able to follow your presentation easily. Also, images and graphics in your presentation can symbolize different things in different cultures. For example, the owl is a symbol of foolishness in China, whereas it is a symbol of wisdom in the West. The audience in your case study scenario is fairly homogenous so you don't really need to worry about cultural differences here.

Presentation environment

Before you give your presentation you need to consider the physical environment in which you will be presenting. Ask yourself the following:

- Where will you be giving your presentation – in a lecture theatre or a small room?

- How many people will be in your audience? (If you are talking to a large audience you might need a microphone.)

- Will you need to bring a laptop?

- Will there be a projector in the room?

- What type of lighting will be in the room?

It's always a good idea to familiarize yourself with the room and the hardware you will be using. You might simply need to know where to plug in your projector, but it's always good to know where the power points are before you begin your presentation, rather than looking for them half-way through!

Timing

How long will your presentation be? This might seem obvious, but you need to know how much time you can spend on each slide. A good guideline is to spend approximately one minute per slide and to allow time at the end for discussion. For example, if you expect to have your audience for half an hour, you might allow 20 slides for 20 minutes of presentation and keep 10 minutes for questions and answers at the end.

Writing your plan

Writing your plan can appear daunting at first. What information will you include? What information will you leave out? How long will your presentation be?

You may find it helpful to start by putting your main points in a Word document: use the Outline feature in Word to organize the points into a logical sequence. This will give you a structure for your presentation, which you can then import into PowerPoint.

Word outlines

Writing your outline in a word processor such as Microsoft Word can help you to order and prioritize the ideas that you want to communicate. It will help you to arrange your information into a logical sequence, so that the audience can follow the presentation.

Exercise 2.1: Exporting a Word document to a presentation

1) Open the Word document GGG.DOC that was supplied with this book.

Presenter
■→Denis O'Dwyer, Green Grocer Group

Our Mission Statement
■→Green Grocer Group works with 75 farmers in 23 locations to provide the finest organic fruit and vegetables

Company History
■→The Green Grocer Group was founded in Devon by Johanna O'Brien and Jim Forster
■→Our company philosophy

About Johanna O'Brien
■→Johanna O'Brien worked for a major supermarket chain where she noticed a demand for organic fruit and vegetables
■→This gave her the idea of setting up a company that supplies organic fruit and vegetables

About Jim Forster
■→Jim Forster is an active member of the organic farming community in Devon
■→With a background in both business and farming, he made the ideal business partner

2) In GGG.DOC, choose **File | Send To | Microsoft PowerPoint**.

3) PowerPoint opens a new presentation, with the Word document GGG.doc as its outline.

1 ■ **Presenter**
   • Denis O'Dwyer, Green Grocer Group
2 ▢ **Our Mission Statement**
   • Green Grocer Group works with 75 farmers in 23 locations to provide the finest organic fruit and vegetables
3 ▢ **Company History**
   • The Green Grocer Group was founded in Devon by Johanna O'Brien and Jim Forster
   • Our company philosophy
4 ▢ **About Johanna O'Brien**
   • Johanna O'Brien worked for a major supermarket chain where she noticed a demand for organic fruit and vegetables

4) Choose **File | Save** and save this presentation as EX2.1.PPT.

Congratulations! You now have the outline of your presentation.

*Merging information
from other presentations*

You can sometimes save time by recycling parts of presentations that either you or your colleagues have previously made. You can easily merge slides from one presentation into another. How? Take a look at the following exercise.

Exercise 2.2: Merging slides from other presentations

1) Open EX2.1.PPT.

2) In the Outline pane, place your cursor at the end of the last bullet point in slide 1, titled 'Presenter'.

> 1 ☐ **Presenter**
>   • Denis O'Dwyer, Green Grocer
>   Group|

3) Choose **Insert | Slides from Files**.

4) Under the **Find Presentation** tab, click the **Browse** button to find PREVIOUS.PPT. (This is the presentation with the slides you want to recycle.)

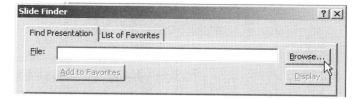

Select the presentation and click **Open**.

5) In the *Select Slides* section, select the second slide, titled 'Green Grocer Group'.

Click the **Insert** button and then click **Close**. (If you want to insert all the slides in a presentation, click the **Insert All** button – but that's not needed here!)

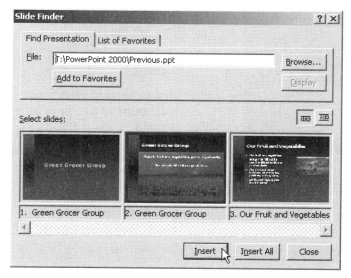

PowerPoint inserts the slide into your presentation after the cursor point. Note that while the content of the new slide comes from the old presentation, it loses its original formatting and needs to be adjusted.

6) Adjust Slide 2, 'Green Grocer Group', so that the graphic fits the slide properly:

- Choose **Format | Slide Layout**.

- Select the *Title Only* layout in the *Slide Layout* dialog box.

- Click **Apply**.

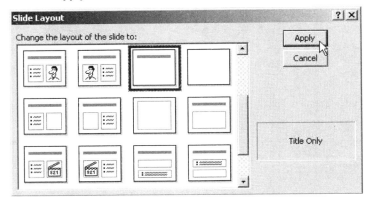

Well done! You've merged a slide from one presentation into another. It looks good doesn't it? And it didn't take too much time!

Making text presentable

Now that you've got your outline, you must make it 'presentable'. How do you do that? There are a few important points that you must keep in mind when preparing your text:

- Break up your information into 'bite-sized' pieces. Concise 'bites' of information are better suited to screen display.

- With text, less is more: if your audience are reading, then they are not listening!

- Use the slides to complement what you are saying, not to repeat it.

- Don't overload your slide. As a guide, restrict each slide to a maximum of five lines of text.

Less is definitely more in PowerPoint presentations. A slide with too much text looks ugly. Nothing puts an audience off more than looking at a 'wall of words' on a slide.

You want your audience to listen to you. Don't distract them by giving them the complete text of your speech on the slide. People will at least scan each new PowerPoint slide you show – by looking at the slide titles and then skimming through the content. Only show enough at a time to reinforce your spoken words.

Research shows that our short-term memory can hold a maximum of five to nine pieces of information. This is the limit of your audience's attention span. (If you want to find out more, read George A. Miller's article 'The Magical Number Seven, Plus or Minus Two: Some Limits on Our Capacity for Processing Information' (www.well.com/user/smalin/miller.html).) Never present more than nine pieces of information on a slide, and for safety, limit yourself to five.

So, how do you apply the 7±2 rule to a PowerPoint presentation? It's quite easy really. You:

- Limit the number of lines per slide to 7±2 (for safety, go for 5).
- Limit the number of words per line to 7±2.

Now let's apply the 7±2 rule to our PowerPoint presentation.

Exercise 2.3: Breaking up your information
1) Open EX2.2.PPT.

2) In Outline view, select slide number 7, titled 'What Makes Green Grocer Group?'. There are six pieces of information here that you can divide across two slides.

3) In the Outline pane, put the cursor at the beginning of the fifth bullet point. Select all of bullet point 5 and bullet point 6.

**New Slide
button**

Press **Ctrl+x** to cut the text so that you can paste it to a new slide.

4) Click the **New Slide** button.

5) In the *Slide Layout* dialog box, select the *Text & Clip Art* layout and click **OK**.

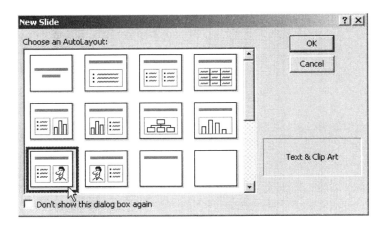

A new slide 8 appears.

6) In the *Click to add text* placeholder, press **Ctrl+v** to paste the selected text to the new slide 8.

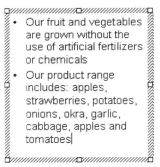

- Our fruit and vegetables are grown without the use of artificial fertilizers or chemicals
- Our product range includes: apples, strawberries, potatoes, onions, okra, garlic, cabbage, apples and tomatoes

7) In slide number 8, type the title of the new slide and centre-align it:

Our Fruit and Vegetables

Our Fruit and Vegetables

8) Double-click the **Clip Art** icon to add a graphic.

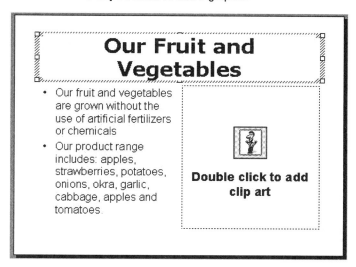

9) In the *Microsoft Clip Gallery* dialog box, type the following piece of text in the *Search for clips* box:

    Vegetables

Scroll down to view the clips of vegetables.

10) Click the graphic of the potatoes and choose **Insert clip** from the menu displayed.

Your slide 8, 'Our Fruit and Vegetables' should look as shown.

Our Fruit and Vegetables

- Our fruit and vegetables are grown without the use of artificial fertilizers or chemicals
- Our product range includes: apples, strawberries, onions, okra, garlic, cabbage, apples and tomatoes

Chapter 2: summary

You must tailor your presentation to the needs of your audience. Choose language, tone, imagery, level of detail and examples that are appropriate.

A *logical sequence* of information will help your audience to understand your presentation better. *Break* your message into small units, each of which contains *7±2* pieces of information. Our *short term memory* imposes limits on our attention span: we cannot handle more than this amount of information at any one time. You may use the *outline* feature in Word to plan your presentation. You can *export* this outline into PowerPoint.

You can also *merge information* on slides from another presentation into your current presentation.

Chapter 2: quick quiz

Circle the correct answer to each of the following questions about the information structure in PowerPoint.

Q1	What would be an appropriate number of slides to use in a 30-minute presentation?
A.	50 slides.
B.	20 slides.
C.	35 slides.
D.	5 slides.

Q2	True or False – our short-term memory can hold a maximum of five to nine pieces of information.
A.	True.
B.	False.

Q3	To merge slides from one presentation into another you choose …
A.	View | Files.
B.	Edit | Files.
C.	Insert | Files.
D.	Format | Files.

Q4	What command do you use to export a Word Outline to PowerPoint?
A.	Edit | Export to | Microsoft PowerPoint.
B.	File | Send to | Microsoft PowerPoint.
C.	Edit | Merge to | Microsoft PowerPoint.
D.	File | Export to | Microsoft PowerPoint.

Answers

1: B, **2:** A, **3:** C, **4:** B.

Design structure

In this chapter

Your presentation might be full of the most interesting, compelling information, but if it is presented in a sloppy, haphazard or unattractive way, you simply won't get your message across. For this reason, you need to give as much attention to the design of your information as to the information itself. Design will either enhance your message or detract from it. Just as you structure the information in your presentation, you also structure its design.

This chapter will focus on the design structure of your presentation – how it can be created using certain PowerPoint features and how it impacts on your audience.

New skills

At the end of this chapter you should be able to:

- Discuss impact of design on the audience
- Choose appropriate font
- Choose appropriate line spacing
- Customize a template
- Create good colour contrast
- Customize a colour scheme
- Customize background fill
- Customize bullet points

New words

At the end of this chapter you should be able to explain the following terms:

- Design template
- Colour wheel
- Colour blindness

Syllabus reference	This chapter covers the following syllabus points: ■ AM 6.1.2.1 ■ AM 6.1.2.2 ■ AM 6.2.1.1 ■ AM 6.2.1.4 ■ AM 6.3.1.3

Impact of design on the audience

Design can have a profound impact on how your audience perceives your message. There are many aspects to design, but here we will focus on just two: font choice and colour choice.

Choosing your font

Although PowerPoint offers you hundreds of fonts to choose from, it's best to limit yourself to one or two in any presentation. If you use more, you run the risk of distracting your audience. Just as consistency in terminology strengthens your presentation, so too does consistency in the use of fonts.

To serif or not serif?

What font should you use in a presentation? Should you use serif fonts such as Times New Roman or sans serif fonts such as Verdana?

- T Verdana
- T Times New Roman

Serif fonts were first developed in Roman times where they were painted on stone and then carved. They are particularly suited to printed text, as the serifs 'bind' the letters into recognizable word shapes, and thus aid legibility. However, in projected material, the serifs tend to blur the letters and result in text that is less readable. Therefore, it is advisable to use sans serif fonts in presentations, as they are easier to read.

Appropriate font size

Your choice of font size depends on two things:

- The size of the screen you will be projecting onto.
- The distance of the audience from this screen.

The minimum legibility standard is one inch (2.5 cm) of letter height on screen for a viewing distance of 30 feet (9 m). This means that in typical situations, 18 points on your computer screen is the absolute minimum. If you suspect that your room will be bigger than normal, or your screen particularly small, choose a larger font size. If in doubt, go large!

Your choice of font size for any piece of text should reflect its relative importance within the presentation: for example Verdana 36 point bold for title text and Arial 28 point for first-level bullets. Once you've chosen these fonts, keep them consistent throughout the presentation.

Adjusting line spacing

Line spacing is the space between one line of text and the next. In PowerPoint you can:

- Change the space between lines in a given paragraph.

- Change the space before a paragraph.

- Change the space after a paragraph.

By adjusting line spacing you can separate the different parts of the text on the slide, and bind together items that you want to bring together. The following exercise shows you how to adjust the line spacing on the Slide Master of your presentation. These changes will affect all line spacing within the presentation.

Exercise 3.1: Adjusting line spacing

1) Open EX3.1.PPT.

2) Choose **View | Master | Slide Master**.

3) Select all levels of the *Master text styles*.

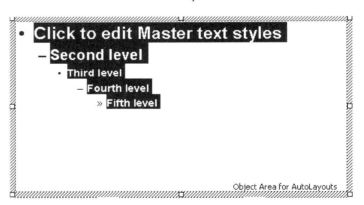

4) Choose **Format | Line Spacing**.

5) In the *Line Spacing* dialog box change:

- *Line spacing* to 1 lines

- *Before paragraph* to 0.5 lines

- *After paragraph* to 0 lines

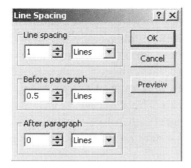

Click **OK**.

Your slide should look as shown.

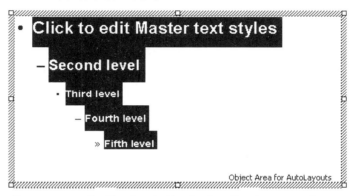

You can press the **Preview** button to view the changes and press **Cancel** if you are not happy with your choices.

Choosing colour

Audience perception can be 'coloured' by:

- Colour response
- Colour blindness
- Colour visibility

Colour response

Some colours and combinations of colours are pleasing to the eye whereas others are literally eyesores. Your choice of colour can provoke both a physical and an emotional response from your audience. For example, while yellow is the most visible colour in the spectrum, it needs to be used sparingly, as it can over-stimulate the eye and result in fatigue. The cultural significance of colour varies from country to country: for example, white is the colour of mourning in China and Japan, whereas in the West, we associate white with birth and new beginnings.

Colour blindness

Some members of your audience are likely to be affected by colour blindness. Colour blindness affects 8% of men, and 0.5% of women. People who are colour blind have difficulties perceiving the difference between certain colours. The most common form of colour blindness affects the ability to perceive green. These people might miss out on valuable information if you rely on colour to convey it. Steer clear of highlighting important issues in green, or making your hyperlinks green.

Colour visibility

It's important to use colours and colour combinations that the audience can see from a distance. After all, your information will appear, not on a printed page, but on a screen, and people will be sitting some distance away from it. The contrast between the colour of the text and the colour of the background of the slide will affect visibility too.

With all this information on colour in mind, let's look at a design template in PowerPoint. Remember, you want to use a template that will have a positive impact on the audience, that will not present problems for colour-blind audience members, and that will be highly visible when on screen.

Design templates

A template is something that serves as a model or example. You use a design template in PowerPoint to serve as a model for all the slides in your presentation.

Design template

A PowerPoint file that can be applied to a PowerPoint presentation to control its principal design elements. A template contains a colour scheme and one or more slide masters with font settings and possibly built-in graphics and text. PowerPoint templates have the file extension .pot.

The great thing about PowerPoint is that it comes with several built-in design templates. You can use them as they appear in PowerPoint, or you can customize them to suit your own needs. Let's open a design template and customize it to suit your presentation.

Exercise 3.2: Customizing a design template

1) Open EX3.2.POT.

2) Choose **Format | Apply Design Template**.

3) In the *Apply Design Template* dialog box, there is a list of available templates. Select the *Azure* template and click **Apply**.

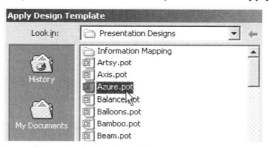

Your slides should look as shown.

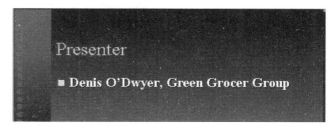

4) Choose **View | Master | Slide Master** and highlight the *Master title style*. Change the font, font size and weight to the following:

> Verdana, 44 point, Bold.

(Remember, sans serif fonts work better in projected materials.)

5) Highlight the first level of the *Master text style* and change the font, font size and weight to the following:

> Arial, 32 point, Bold.

6) Highlight the second level of the *Master text style* and change the font, font size and weight to the following:

Arial, 28 point, Bold.

7) Move the *Master title style* box to the very top of the slide by clicking its outline and moving it up. (Notice how your cursor has changed to a four-headed cross?)

Line button

8) Click the **Line** button on the *Drawing* toolbar to add a line underneath the *Master title style* box.

Keep the **Shift** button pressed down as you draw a line under the box as shown. (This ensures that the line is perfectly horizontal.)

9) Copy the line underneath the *Master text style* box by selecting it and pressing **Ctrl+c** and **Ctrl+v**.

Drag and drop the new line below the *Object Area for AutoLayouts*.

Your slide master should now look as shown.

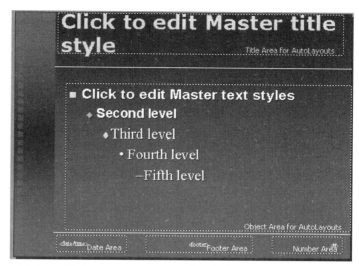

Well done! You've customized your first design template. You'll customize it further as you go through the rest of the chapter.

Your colour scheme should help to communicate your message by making it easier to read, and by giving a consistent look and feel to your presentation.

Each design template in PowerPoint has its own colour scheme. These colour schemes have a range of coordinated colours for background, fill colour, hyperlinks and so on. You can customize these colour schemes to suit yourself. However, it's best to restrict your colour scheme to two or three colours. Too many colours compete for attention and can distract your audience. The following exercise shows you how to customize a colour scheme.

Exercise 3.3: Customizing colour schemes

1) Open EX3.3.POT.

2) Choose **Format | Slide Color Scheme**.

3) Under the **Standard** tab, select the colour scheme that is nearest the one that you want. For our purposes, let's choose the dark blue scheme.

Chapter 3: Design structure

21

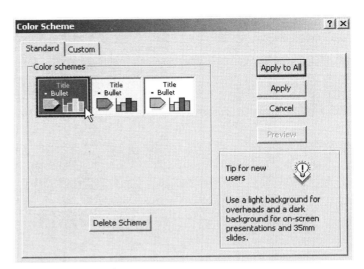

4) Click the **Custom** tab.

5) Under *Scheme colors* select the *Accent and hyperlink* option. You want to change it from mauve to yellow. Click the **Change Color** button.

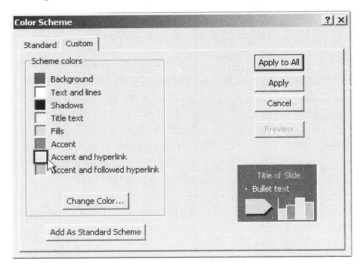

6) Under the **Standard** tab, select a bright yellow colour, and click **OK**.

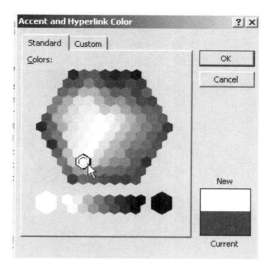

7) Select the *Fills* option. Click the **Change Color** button.

8) Under the **Standard** tab, select the grey colour at the bottom of the dialog box, and click **OK**.

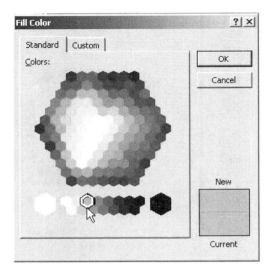

9) Click **Apply to All**. PowerPoint applies the new colours to all the slides in the presentation.

Colour contrast refers to the degree to which elements in the presentation stand out from each other. Colour contrast is important because it affects the audience's ability to view and read your presentation.

For our presentation, let's work with the dark blue background and change the font colour for the title text to a soft yellow. In presentations it's good to use light text on a dark background (unlike in printed material).

Yellow is a good choice for a font colour as experts say it is the first colour that the human eye notices. It draws attention to the text and temporarily wakes your brain up!

Dark blue is a good background colour. Yellow and blue are also primary colours; they make a strong combination.

In the next exercise, modify the template to present the title text in yellow.

Exercise 3.4: Customizing font colour to create greater contrast

1) Open EX3.4.POT.

2) Choose **View | Master | Slide Master**.

3) Select the *Title Style* placeholder, then click the arrow to the right of the **Font Color** button on the *Drawing* toolbar.

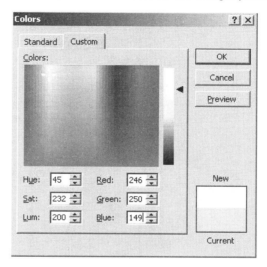

Click to edit Master title style

A ▾

4) Click the *More Font Colors* option and select the **Custom** tab. Use the cross hairs to select your colour and use the slider to adjust the luminosity. For the exercise, choose a bright yellow colour.

To ensure consistency in your colour scheme you can input the values directly into the *Colors* dialog box (as shown above). Click **OK**.

5) Click **Save**.

Customize bullet points

You can customize the bullet points in the slide master in two ways: by changing their shape and by changing their colour. If you want to change the type of bullet point, you choose **Format | Bullets and Numbering** and select the bullet style you want to use.

The following exercise will show you how to change the bullet point colour but you will keep the default bullet types.

Exercise 3.5: Customizing the colour of bullet points
1) Open EX3.5.POT.

2) Choose **View | Master | Slide Master**.

3) Highlight all the master text styles on the slide master.

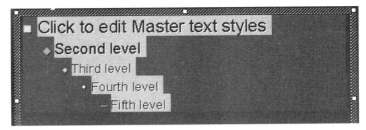

4) Choose **Format | Bullets and Numbering**.

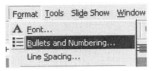

5) Under the **Bulleted** tab click the arrow to the right of the *Color* box. Our custom yellow colour is displayed in the **Color** menu. Place your cursor on the colour and click it. This changes the colour of the bullet points to light yellow.

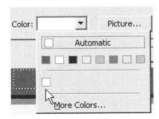

Click **OK**.

Your master slide should look as shown.

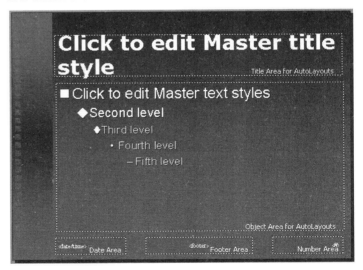

So far, the background of your slides is dark blue. You can change this background colour and you can apply special effects to the background, such as textures, colour gradients, patterns and pictures. To do this choose **Format | Background**. Then click the arrow to the right of the *Background fill* colour box and select the colour or fill effect of your choice. Click **Apply** to change just the current slide, or click **Apply to All** to change all slides in the presentation.

You can also apply a colour and fill effects to a placeholder or drawn object. In the next exercise, you will apply a colour gradient effect to a placeholder in the template's slide master.

Exercise 3.6: Customizing fill colour

1) Open EX3.6.POT.

2) Choose **View | Master | Slide Master**.

3) Click in the title placeholder. Click the arrow to the right of the **Fill Color** button. Select the *Fill Effects* option.

4) Under the **Gradient** tab, select the *Preset* option. Click the arrow to the right of the *Preset Colors* box and select the *Nightfall* option.

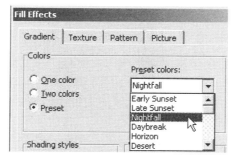

5) Under the *Shading Styles* section, select the *Diagonal up* option. Press OK.

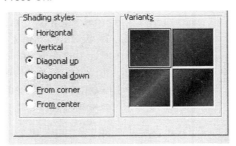

6) Switch to Normal view to look at the changes to your template – choose **View | Normal**.

Other fill effects

Explore the other fill effects available in PowerPoint, such as textures, patterns and pictures. Remember, you can access these effects by clicking arrow to the right of the **Fill Color** button.

The **Textures** tab offers a range of textures you can apply to your slides. The texture selected below is of recycled paper.

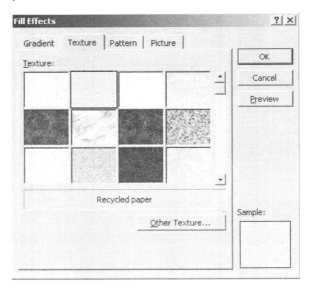

The **Pattern** tab offers a range of patterns as shown below.

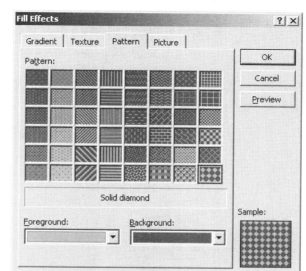

With the **Picture** tab, you can include a picture in your slides, either as a background image or as a unifying design element. You might use this, for example, to include a company logo or symbol in your presentation.

Inserting a logo

Inserting a logo is easy. The following exercise shows you how to insert a logo in the slide master, so that it subsequently appears on each slide in your presentation.

Exercise 3.7: Inserting a logo into your slide master

1) Open EX3.7.POT.

2) Choose **View | Master | Slide Master**.

3) Choose **Insert | Picture | From File**.

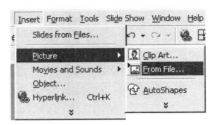

4) Navigate to where you have stored your company logo GGG.JPG. Click **Insert**.

5) Drag and drop the logo to the *Date Area* box.

6) Save the template as CAPRI.POT.

   ■ Choose **File | Save As** and type the following in the *File name* box:

      Capri

   ■ In the *Save as type* box, select *Design Template*.

   ■ In the *Save in* box, select the location where you want to save your template.

   ■ Click **Save**.

Applying the design template

So far you've created a new design template and customized it to suit your needs. Now, all that remains for you to do is to apply your new template to a presentation.

Exercise 3.8: Applying the design template

1) Open EX3.8.PPT.

2) Choose **Format | Apply Design Template**.

3) In the *Apply Design Template* box, navigate to where you have stored CAPRI.POT.

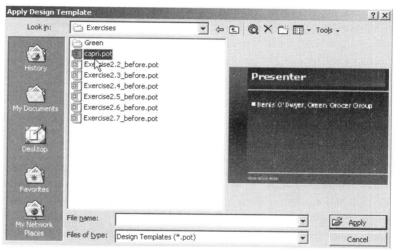

4) Select CAPRI.POT and click **Apply**.

Congratulations! You've now applied a template to your presentation. Notice how each slide in the presentation has adopted the colour scheme and font characteristics that you specified in the template, and has the logo in the bottom-left corner.

Title slide

There's just one more thing to do. This presentation does not yet include a title slide: you will have to insert one yourself and adjust its design to make it consistent with the other slides.

A title slide is the first slide in your presentation, and it may also be used at other points to introduce a new topic or section. It is normally formatted differently from the rest of the slides in your presentation, while retaining the same basic design elements. In the following exercises, you will insert a title slide and change some of its design features.

Exercise 3.9: Inserting a title slide

1) Open EX3.9.PPT.

2) In the Outline pane, place your cursor before the text of slide 1, titled 'Presenter'.

> 1 ☐ Presenter
> • Denis O'Dwyer, Green Grocer
>   Group

3) Click the **New Slide** button, and select the *Title Slide* slide layout in the *New Slide* dialog box. Click **OK**.

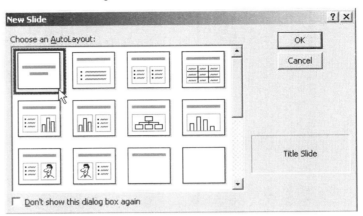

The title slide now appears as slide 1.

4) Type the following title in the *Master title style* placeholder:

Green Grocer Group

5) Choose the following font, size, style, positioning and colour:

Verdana, 48 point, Bold, Centred, White.

6) Select the *Click to add subtitle* box. Choose **Insert | Picture | From File**.

7) Navigate to where you have saved the logo of Organic Farming in Europe – ORGANICS.JPG, and click **OK**.

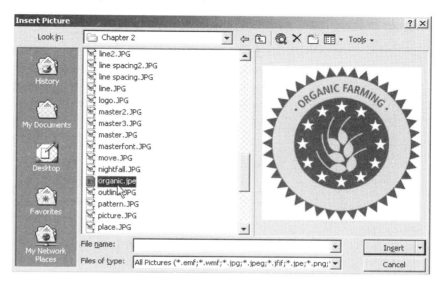

The graphic now appears on your slide.

8) Resize the *Subtitle* box so that it fits the logo as shown.

Well done! You've successfully created a title slide. To subsequently change any of the elements or characteristics of the title slide, choose **View | Master | Title Master**.

Each element in your slide – text, drawn object, imported picture – is on a separate 'layer'. A slide might have several layers – a number of text boxes on an imported diagram, for example, or a background photograph behind your text, or a drawing consisting of a square, a triangle and a circle. The order in which these layers are drawn by PowerPoint can be changed to create different effects – you can make the elements overlap in different ways. You will need to do this particularly if you have complex graphics with explanatory text. When you select any object, PowerPoint offers you the following options:

- **Bring to Front** (bring the selected object to the front of the stack).

- **Send to Back** (send the selected object to the back of the stack).

- **Bring Forward** (bring the selected object one layer forward in the stack).

- **Send Backward** (send the selected object one layer backward in the stack).

These options are available from the **Draw** menu on the *Drawing* toolbar.

Exercise 3.10: Apply stacking effects to the title slide

1) Open EX3.10.PPT, and go to the first slide.

2) Click the **Rectangle** button on the *Drawing* toolbar and place a rectangle over the Green Grocer Group title.

Your title is now covered by the rectangle.

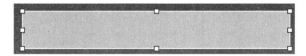

3) Choose **Draw | Order | Send to Back** from the *Drawing* toolbar.

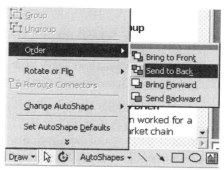

Notice that the rectangle has moved behind the text – the text can now be read, and the rectangle provides contrast.

Green Grocer Group

Exercise 3.11: Apply stacking effects to a picture or image

1) Open EX3.10.PPT, and go to the second slide, 'Presenter'.

2) Click at the start of the bulleted text 'Denis ...'. Press ENTER five times to move the text down the slide.

3) Click below the text or outside the text box. Notice that the picture obscures part of the text.

4) Select the picture and choose **Draw | Order | Send to Back** from the *Drawing* toolbar.

Notice that the picture is now behind the text, and the text is now readable.

Chapter 3: summary

Consider the *audience* and the presentation *environment* before you decide on your design: the various design elements – font size and style, colour scheme, use of graphics, and so on – must be chosen with these in mind. Design with the audience's needs in mind, because if you make it easy for them to see your slides, you have a better chance of getting your message across. Remember that colour has a profound physical and emotional impact on an audience – and that you cannot take everything for granted: cultural differences may affect how your message is perceived, and physical differences (poor eyesight, colour blindness) may impede the understanding of some of your audience.

Choose a point size that is suitable for the room in which you will be presenting. As a guide, never use type smaller than 18 point. For presentations, it is recommended to use a sans serif font, such as Arial or Verdana. And control *line spacing* so that each point appears both coherent and separate.

Your *colour scheme* should ensure a strong contrast between the foreground and the background. It is recommended to use a dark colour (such as navy blue) for the background and a light colour (such as bright yellow) for the text.

PowerPoint's *design templates* give you a basis on which to model your presentation. You can *customize* the design templates to your own requirements, by changing any of the elements in the Slide Master or Title Master, such as the fonts, the bullet characters, and the colour scheme. You can further customize the *background* by adding gradients, textures and pictures (such as logos).

When the template is customized to your satisfaction, you *apply* it to your presentation.

Stacking objects on your slides allows you to control how elements on your slide appear in relation to one another. You can move objects backwards or forwards on a slide so that they overlap in the way that you want.

Chapter 3: quick quiz

Circle the correct answer to each of the following questions about the design structure in PowerPoint 2000.

Q1	Which of the following statements about the Design Template are untrue?
A.	The Design Template has the file extension .pot.
B.	The Design Template cannot be customized.
C.	The Design Template comes with a title master and a slide master.
D.	The Design Template comes with a built-in colour scheme.

Q2	Which of the following is not an appropriate font size for a PowerPoint presentation?
A.	17 point.
B.	22 point.
C.	28 point.
D.	32 point.

Q3	To customize a colour scheme you …
A.	Choose **Format | Slide Color Scheme**. Under the **Custom** tab, select the components that you want to customize and click the Change Color button. Select the color you need and click **OK** and then press **Apply to All**.
B.	Choose **Format | Slide Color Scheme**. Under the **Standard** tab, select the components that you want to customize and click the **Change Color** button. Select the color you need and click **OK** and then press **Apply to All**.
C.	Choose **Format | Slide Color Scheme**. Under the **Custom** tab, select the components that you want to customize and click the **Add as Standard Scheme** button. Select the color you need and click **OK** and then press **Apply to All**.
D.	Choose **Format | Slide Color Scheme**. Under the **Custom** tab, select the components that you want to customize and click the **Change Color** button. Select the color you need and click **OK**.

Q4	Choose the sans serif font below.
A.	Times New Roman.
B.	Courier.
C.	Verdana.
D.	Garamond.

Answers

1: B, **2:** A, **3:** A, **4:** C.

Flowcharts

In this chapter

In this chapter you will create a flowchart to illustrate a series of actions and decisions. Flowcharts are useful tools for detailing the different steps needed in order to complete an action. In your presentation, you will use a flowchart to show the different steps in the organic certification process.

New skills

At the end of this chapter you should be able to:

- Insert the appropriate AutoShapes needed for a flowchart
- Position and resize a shape
- Insert text in an AutoShape
- Adjust text to fit an AutoShape
- Align AutoShapes
- Insert connector lines and arrows
- Insert text boxes

New words

At the end of this chapter you should be able to explain the following terms:

- Flowchart
- AutoShape
- Connectors

Syllabus reference

This chapter covers the following syllabus points:

- AM 6.3.1.2
- AM 6.3.1.4
- AM 6.3.1.5

- AM 6.3.2.4
- AM 6.4.2.1
- AM 6.4.2.2
- AM 6.4.2.3

The **Drawing** *toolbar*

The two main menus on PowerPoint's *Drawing* toolbar are:

- The **AutoShapes** menu
- The **Draw** menu

You use the **AutoShapes** menu to create the shapes you need for a flowchart, and you use the **Draw** menu to position these shapes.

There are other useful options available from the *Drawing* toolbar, such as:

- The **3-D** button
- The **Text box** button

These options can really add visual excitement to your flowchart and make it stand out. That said, remember that 'less is more' – be selective in your use of effects options. For example, don't add a 3-D effect to all the text and AutoShapes in a flowchart, as this may make the flowchart less legible.

Parts of a flowchart

The principal shapes used in a flowchart are:

Shape	Name	Purpose
▭	Rectangle (Process)	Indicates an action
◇	Diamond (Decision)	Indicates a question or decision
▢	Oval (Terminator)	Indicates where a process begins and ends

These parts are connected by lines or arrows to indicate the flow.

Now that you know what is involved, you can begin to create your own flowchart.

Exercise 4.1 Beginning a flowchart

1) Open EX4.1.PPT. Go to slide number 13, 'Organic Certification Process'.

2) Choose **AutoShapes | Flowchart** from the *Drawing* toolbar.

3) Click the shape labelled Terminator (third row, first on left).

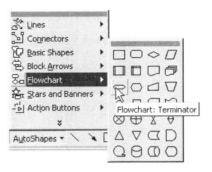

4) Click near the top left-hand corner of the slide and drag to create a terminator shape as shown.

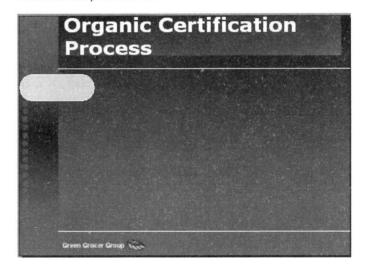

If necessary, reposition the AutoShape by clicking in it and then dragging it.

Another way to reposition an AutoShape is to use specific co-ordinates. The following exercise shows you how apply co-ordinates to a terminator.

Exercise 4.2: Working on the terminators

1) Open EX4.2.PPT. Go to slide number 13, 'Organic Certification Process'.

2) Select the terminator and press **Ctrl+c** to copy it. Press **Ctrl+v** to paste it to the slide.

3) Reposition the new terminator, this time by specifying co-ordinates. Right-click the new terminator and choose *Format AutoShape*. Under the **Position** tab, input the *Position on slide* information as shown below. Click **OK**.

The new shape now appears at the bottom-right of the slide as shown below.

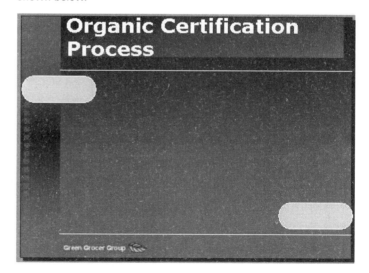

Now let's add more AutoShapes to the flowchart and then format their positioning and size.

You want to add more shapes to your flowchart. You need a rectangle for each step in the process, and a diamond shape for each decision. Make these shapes approximately the same size, and place them on the slide. (If you make a mistake, simply delete the AutoShape and start again, as in the exercise below.)

Exercise 4.3: Adding different AutoShapes

1) Open EX4.3.PPT. Go to slide number 13, 'Organic Certification Process'.

2) Select the first terminator and choose **Edit | Duplicate** (**Ctrl+d**). A second oval appears. However, you want a diamond, as you will be illustrating a decision step.

3) Choose **Draw | Change AutoShape | Flowchart** from the *Drawing* toolbar. Click the decision diamond shape at the top of the menu.

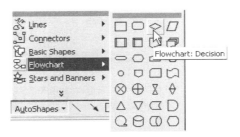

The new oval changes to a diamond.

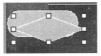

4) Drag the diamond to the middle of the slide. Your slide should look as shown.

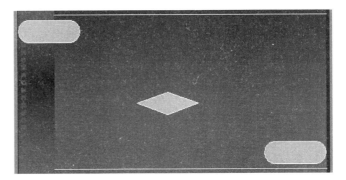

5) Duplicate the diamond by selecting it and pressing **Ctrl+d**.

6) Choose **Draw | Change AutoShape | Flowchart** and click the rectangle shape at the top of the menu.

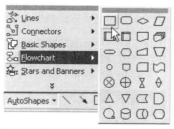

The duplicated diamond changes to a rectangle.

7) Duplicate this rectangle three more times so that there are now four rectangles on the slide.

8) Drag the new shapes into position as shown below.

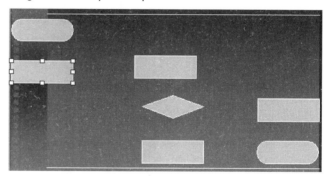

Fantastic! You've created all the AutoShapes that you need for your flowchart.

Deleting AutoShapes: to delete an object from a PowerPoint slide, select it and press **Delete**. Try this on one of the AutoShapes in the slide you   have created, and then choose **Edit | Undo Clear** to restore it (or press **Ctrl + z**).

You now need to 'tidy up' the AutoShapes on the slide. You can do this by using the **Align or Distribute** feature on the *Drawing* toolbar. This enables you to align AutoShapes relative to each other. For example, if you want to align AutoShapes horizontally by their centres, click **Align Center**. You can also arrange AutoShapes at equal distances from each other, relative to the slide. You simply select the AutoShapes and choose **Draw | Align or Distribute| Relative to Slide** and select the distribute function that you need: **Distribute Horizontally** or **Distribute Vertically**.

The following exercise shows you how to align the different AutoShapes on a flowchart.

Exercise 4.4: Aligning AutoShapes

1) Open EX.4.4.PPT. Go to slide number 13, 'Organic Certification Process'.

2) Select the three AutoShapes in the middle of the slide: the two rectangles and the diamond. (Hold down the **Shift** key and click each of the shapes in turn.)

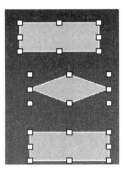

3) Choose **Draw | Align or Distribute | Align Center** from the *Drawing* toolbar. This aligns the AutoShapes by their centres, as shown.

4) Select the top-left rectangle and the top-centre rectangle as shown.

5) Choose **Draw | Align or Distribute | Align Middle** from the *Drawing* toolbar. This aligns the AutoShapes by their middles, as shown.

6) Select the bottom oval and the right-hand rectangle as shown.

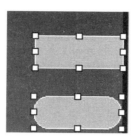

7) Choose **Draw | Align or Distribute | Align Centre** from the *Drawing* toolbar. This aligns the AutoShapes by their centres, as shown.

Well done! You've aligned the AutoShapes. Your slide should now look as shown.

Now, your next step is to add some colour to the chart. Why don't you change the background colour of the AutoShapes? You can do this by using grouping techniques.

Grouping techniques

PowerPoint enables you to treat a group of objects as a single entity, and to apply effects to the group as a whole. This technique saves you time and effort, as you only need to apply one effect to cover all the shapes in the group. It also helps to ensure consistency throughout your flowchart.

The next exercise shows you how to group AutoShapes in order to apply colour effects.

Exercise 4.5: Grouping AutoShapes to apply colour effects

1) Open EX4.5.PPT. Go to slide number 13, 'Organic Certification Process'.

2) Select all the AutoShapes except the ovals by holding down the **Shift** key and clicking each of the shapes in turn.

Shift key

3) Choose **Draw | Group** from the *Drawing* toolbar. This groups the AutoShapes together, so that any action applied to one shape will automatically be applied to every shape.

4) Click the arrow to the right of the **Fill Color** button. Select the *Fill Effects* option.

5) Under the **Gradient** tab, select the *Two colors* option. Select light grey as *Color 1* and white as *Color 2*.

6) Under *Shading styles* choose the *Diagonal up* option. Click **OK**.

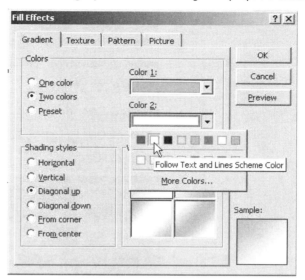

Your flowchart should look as shown.

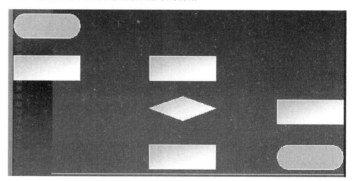

7) Choose **Draw | Ungroup** from the *Drawing* toolbar. Each shape is now independent.

What else do we need to put into the flowchart? Why, text of course, otherwise your audience won't be able to understand your flowchart!

Adding text to AutoShapes

Adding text to an AutoShape is easy. Make sure that your text is small enough to fit in the AutoShape but large enough to read. (Remember the 18 point minimum that we discussed in Chapter 3.)

Exercise 4.6: Adding text to AutoShapes

1) Open EX4.6.PPT. Go to slide number 13, 'Organic Certification Process'.

2) Type the following pieces of text into the AutoShapes:

Terminator 1: `Start`

Rectangle 1: `Submit application to agency`

Rectangle 2: `Organic Inspection`

Diamond: `Satisfactory?`

Rectangle 3: `Correct and resubmit`

Rectangle 4: `Certification`

Terminator 2: `End`

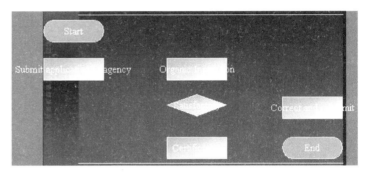

The font colour makes the flowchart hard to read doesn't it? Let's amend the text.

3) Group the AutoShapes again: select all the shapes and choose **Draw | Group**.

4) Change the font to Arial, 18 point, Bold, Black.

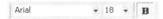

Note that the text in all the AutoShapes has changed font and colour.

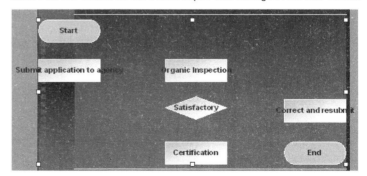

5) Choose **Draw | Ungroup** from the *Drawing* toolbar.

Note that the text in the shapes does not fit. Don't panic – you can adjust both the text and the size of the AutoShape.

Exercise 4.7: Adjusting text and AutoShapes

1) Open EX4.7.PPT. Go to slide number 13, 'Organic Certification Process'.

2) Select the top-left rectangle.

3) Place your cursor between the two words 'application' and 'to' and press **Enter**.

4) With the same rectangle selected, position the cursor on one of the corner handles.

Drag the double-headed arrow to enlarge the rectangle so that it accommodates the text.

5) Apply similar changes to the remaining shapes.

Your slide should look as shown.

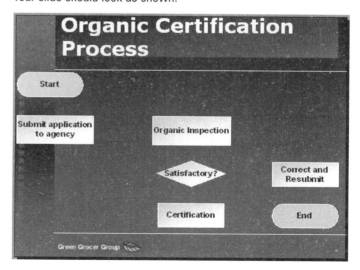

Arrows

In a flowchart, the flow is normally from top to bottom and left to right, in which case the shapes can be connected by a simple line. If the flow is in any other direction, the shapes must be connected by an arrow.

PowerPoint offers you two line options:

■ The **Line** button on the *Drawing* toolbar.

■ The **Connectors** option in the **AutoShapes** menu.

PowerPoint offers you three arrow options:

■ The **Arrow** button on the *Drawing* toolbar.

■ The **Block Arrows** option in the **AutoShapes** menu.

■ The **Connectors** option in the **AutoShapes** menu.

You are probably already familiar with the **Line** button and the **Arrow** button on the *Drawing* toolbar but perhaps not so familiar with the **Connectors** option. In the following exercises you will add arrows and connectors to the flowchart.

Exercise 4.8: Adding arrows to a flowchart

1) Open EX4.8.PPT. Go to slide number 13, 'Organic Certification Process'.

2) Click the **Arrow** button on the *Drawing* toolbar.

Arrow
button

3) Draw an arrow between the first terminator and the rectangle beneath it, as shown.

4) Duplicate the arrow (**Ctrl+d**).

5) Drag the new arrow and position it between the centre rectangle and the diamond. Adjust its length to make it fit, as shown.

6) Add five more arrows to your flowchart:

- One arrow between the diamond and the rectangle below it.

- One arrow between the two top rectangles.

- One arrow between the diamond and the right-hand rectangle.

- One arrow between the bottom rectangle and the end terminator.

- One arrow between the right-hand rectangle and the second rectangle at the top.

Your flowchart should now look as shown.

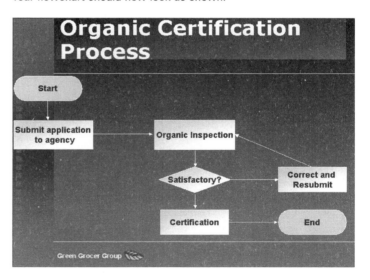

To complete your flowchart, you need to do two things:

- Add text to indicate the flow from the decision diamond.

- Use a connector line instead of the rather inelegant arrow joining the 'Correct and Resubmit' box to the 'Organic Inspection' box.

In the next exercise you will add two text boxes – one beside each of the arrows leading from the decision diamond.

Exercise 4.9: Adding text boxes to a flowchart

1) Open EX4.9.PPT. Go to slide number 13, 'Organic Certification Process'.

2) Click the **Text Box** button on the *Drawing* toolbar.

3) Draw a text box beside the diamond as shown.

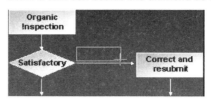

4) Type 'N' in the text box.

   Change the font to Arial, 18 point, Bold.

   Your text box should look as shown.

5) Similarly, draw a text box between the diamond and the bottom rectangle, with the letter 'Y' in it.

   Your text boxes should now look as shown.

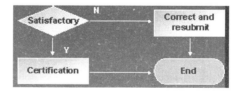

Connector lines

A connector is a special kind of line used to connect two flowchart shapes. The line 'sticks' to the shape even when the shape changes position and it's able to find the shortest route between the two shapes.

Connector lines can be straight, elbowed or curved, and they can have no arrow, an arrow at one end, or an arrow at each end. For flowcharting purposes, the best choice is:

■ Elbowed

■ One arrow

To draw a connector line, choose **AutoShapes | Connectors**, select the connector you want to use, click in the first shape you want to connect and then click in the second shape. Notice that four blue squares appear on the AutoShape itself; these are the possible attachment points for the connector.

When drawing a connector line, you will notice that the handles at the ends of the line change colour:

- Green: ending is not attached to a shape.

- Red: ending is attached to a shape.

If your connector has a yellow handle at its mid point, you can use this to change the shape of the connector without detaching it.

You can detach a connector line and 'reroute' it to another AutoShape: select it and then drag its handle (red or green) to the new shape.

Exercise 4.10: Working with connector lines

1) Open EX4.10.PPT. Go to slide number 13, 'Organic Certification Process'.

2) Delete the arrow joining the 'Correct and Resubmit' box to the 'Organic Inspection' box.

3) Select the rectangle with the text 'Correct and resubmit'.

4) Choose **AutoShapes | Connectors** from the *Drawing* toolbar. Click the *Curved Arrow Connector* option.

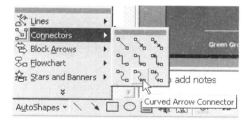

5) Draw a connector from the right-hand rectangle to the centre rectangle as shown.

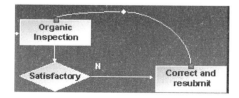

6) Curved connectors are not normally used in flowcharts, so let's change the connector type.

Right-click the connector and choose **Elbow Connector**.

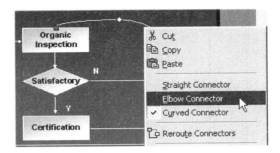

Your connector has now changed to an elbowed line.

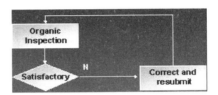

Chapter 4: summary

A *flowchart* is the graphical representation of a series of actions and decisions needed for a particular task or procedure. You use the following AutoShapes to create a flowchart: *diamonds*, *terminators* and *rectangles*.

Arrows or *connector lines* are used to link each shape in the flowchart. Position your shapes on a chart either by *dragging* the shape to the desired location or by using *specific coordinates*. Distribute the AutoShapes evenly by using the **Align or Distribute** option.

Group the AutoShapes together in order to apply effects to all of them. You can heighten the impact of your flowchart by introducing different colours, for example by adding a *graduated colour* to an AutoShape. You will need to *add text* to the AutoShapes and probably need to put *text boxes* into your flowchart to add extra information outside of the shapes. You can *adjust* the AutoShape to fit the text by stretching it.

Chapter 4: quick quiz

Circle the correct answer to each of the following questions on flowcharts.

Q1	What shape do you use for the start and end of a flowchart?
A.	◇
B.	⬭
C.	▭
D.	○

Q2	What shape do you use for a decision step in a flowchart?
A.	◇
B.	⬭
C.	▭
D.	○

Q3	Using specific coordinates, how do you position a shape in a flow chart?
A.	Right-click the shape and choose **Set AutoShapes Default** from the menu. Under the **Position** tab, input the *Position on Slide* information.
B.	Right-click the shape and choose **Format AutoShape** from the menu. Under the **Picture** tab, input the *Position on Slide* information.
C.	Right-click the shape and choose **Set AutoShapes Default** from the menu. Under the **Position** tab, input the *Scale* information.
D.	Right-click the shape and choose **Format AutoShape** from the menu. Under the **Position** tab, input the *Position on Slide* information.

Q4	True or false – a connector line 'sticks' to a shape even when the shape changes position.
A.	True.
B.	False.

Q5	What shortcut command do you use to duplicate a shape in a flowchart?
A.	Ctrl+c.
B.	Ctrl+v.
C.	Ctrl+d.
D.	Ctrl+v.

Answers

1: B, **2:** A, **3:** D, **4:** A, **5:** C.

5

Charts

In this chapter

Creating a good chart takes time and effort, but it's worth this investment. Charts help your audience to understand quantitative (number-based) information at a glance.

Keep your chart as simple as possible:

- Limit yourself to a few colours

- Use the chart as the main mechanism to convey your information – use as little text as possible

- Keep visibility issues in mind – remember the 18 point minimum guideline

New skills

At the end of this chapter you should be able to:

- Import a cell range from Excel

- Create a combination chart

- Change the scale of the value axis

- Change the display of the value axis

- Rotate a 3-D chart

- Elevate a 3-D chart

- Add and adjust labels

New words

At the end of this chapter you should be able to explain the following terms:

- Data series

- Combination chart

- Exploded pie chart

Syllabus reference

This chapter covers the following syllabus points:

- AM 6.4.1.1
- AM 6.4.1.2
- AM 6.4.1.3
- AM 6.4.1.4
- AM 6.4.1.5

Selecting chart types

The main chart types are:

- Column charts
- Bar charts
- Line charts
- Pie charts

So how do you know which type of chart to use?

Column charts

The default chart in PowerPoint is the column chart, in which numbers are represented by vertical bars. Column charts are useful when you want to compare quantities – for example, the sales of bananas in each month of the year, or the population of South American countries.

Bar charts

Bar charts are similar to column charts, except that the bars are horizontal. Bar charts are useful when the bars represent distances or speeds, such as the processing speed of different computers, or the personal best performances of different Olympic long-jump contestants. Bar charts are also useful if the label associated with each bar is lengthy, as the label can fit on a single line beside the bar.

Line charts

Line charts are useful when you want to show trends, such as the changing pattern of cigarette consumption since 1956.

Pie charts

Pie charts represent the parts of a whole as segments of a circle. They are useful when you want to give a break-down of a figure, or show the percentages of a total – for example, the market share of different brands of DVD players.

You want to show your audience some quantitative information. This information might originate in an Excel spreadsheet or an Access database. But no audience wants to look at a wall of figures. For their sake, you should create some visual interest by turning such information into a chart.

If your information comes from Excel, you can import a whole spreadsheet or a range of cells and use the information to build a chart. Let's work with the supplied spreadsheet END OF YEAR RESULTS.XLS. In the following exercise, you will import a cell range that will become the basis for your chart.

Exercise 5.1: Importing a cell range

1) Open EX5.1.PPT. Go to slide number 14, 'End of Year Results'.

2) Choose **Format | Slide Layout**. In the *Slide Layout* dialog box, select the *Chart* slide layout and click **Apply**.

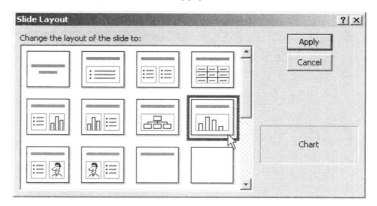

3) Double-click the chart icon. A default chart appears.

4) Choose **Edit | Import File**. Navigate to the Excel Spreadsheet END OF YEAR RESULTS.XLS and double-click it.

5) In the *Import Data Options* dialog box, select Sheet 1.

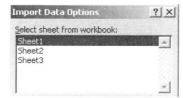

6) In the *Import* section, select the *Range* option.

In the *Range* box, enter the following range of cells:

A2:C5.

7) Select the *Overwrite existing cells* check box. Click **OK**.

The financial results from the spreadsheet are now represented in a column chart.

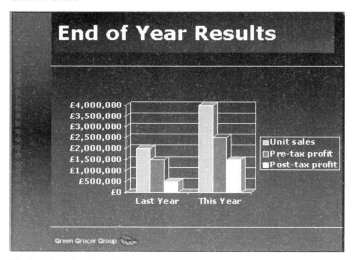

Notice that the datasheet has also changed.

		A	B	C
		Last Year	This Year	
1	Unit sales	2,000,000	4,000,000	
2	Pre-tax pro	£1,500,000	£2,500,000	
3	Post-tax pr	£500,000	£1,500,000	
4				

Well done! You've imported quantitative information (a cell range) and turned it into a column chart.

Combination charts

A combination chart is used to show the relationship between different *kinds* of information. You could use one, for example, to chart ice-cream sales against daily temperature. You can combine any of the different chart types within PowerPoint, but the most common choice is to combine a column chart with a line chart.

The only charts you can combine in PowerPoint are 2-D ones – PowerPoint does not allow you to create 3-D combination charts. (A 3-D combination chart would be potentially confusing.) In the next exercise you will convert your existing 3-D chart to a 2-D combination chart. This chart will contain both a column chart and a line chart.

Up to this point your chart has three data series, each of them shown as a vertical bar. When you convert it to a combination chart, one of the data series – the one relating to unit sales – will be shown as a line.

Exercise 5.2: Creating a combination chart

1) Open EX5.2.PTT. Go to slide number 14, 'End of Year Results'.

2) Double-click the chart so that the datasheet appears.

3) Right-click the chart area. Choose **Chart Type** from the menu that appears.

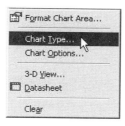

In the **Standard Types** tab, select the first chart sub-type, *Clustered Column*.

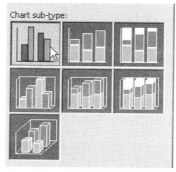

Click **OK**.

The chart is now 2-D.

4) Right-click either of the 'Unit sales' columns. (Unit Sales are represented by the first column in each group.)

Choose **Chart Type** from the menu that appears.

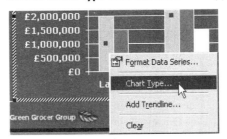

5) In the **Standard Types** tab, select the *Line* chart type.

6) Select the first *Chart sub-type*. This is the chart type used to display trends.

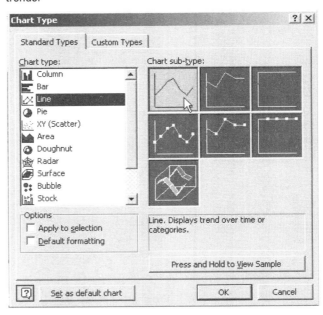

If you want a preview of the combination chart, use the **Press and Hold to View Sample** button. Click the **OK** button.

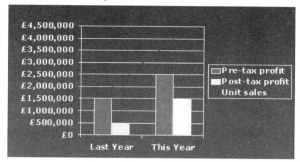

Well done! You have now created a chart that combines both a line chart and a column chart. However, the audience might find the line, in the line chart, hard to see. To make it more visible, change its colour and make it thicker in the following exercise.

Exercise 5.3: Formatting a chart

1) Open EX5.3.PPT. Go to slide number 14, 'End of Year Results'.

2) Double-click the combination chart so that the datasheet appears.

3) Right-click the line in the line chart. Choose **Format Data Series** from the menu.

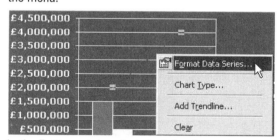

4) In the **Patterns** tab, select the following options:

Under *Line*:

- *Custom*

- *Style*: first option (continuous line)

- *Color*: orange

- *Weight*: last option (thick line)

- *Smoothed line*: select the check box

Under *Marker*:

- *Custom*

- *Foreground*: black

- *Background*: white

- *Style*: diamond (you will not see the diamond until you've changed the colours as above)

- *Size*: 12 point

- *Shadow*: select the check box

Click the **OK** button.

Your chart should look as shown.

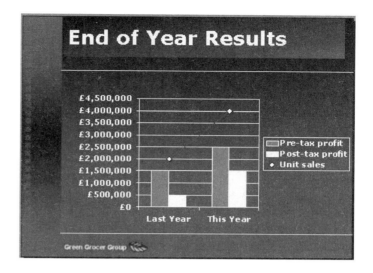

Occupational hazard!

It's an occupational hazard of working with PowerPoint that occasionally your right-clicks are misinterpreted. You might not have clicked on exactly the right place. Go back and try again.

Modifying scales

The Y-axis (vertical axis) in your chart shows the values of sales and profits (for this reason, the Y-axis is also known as the value axis). When the chart is created, PowerPoint allocates default settings to the Y-axis. You can modify these default settings in three ways:

- Change the scale of the Y-axis by specifying a minimum and a maximum value. This is useful if your data consists of high numbers within a narrow range (for example, sales figures, all of which lie between 10 million and 10.5 million). Changing the scale will enable you to highlight the differences.

- Change the units on the Y-axis – such as changing from hundreds to thousands.

- Change the interval between units on the Y-axis to simplify your chart.

Changing the scale of the Y-axis

To change the scale of the Y-axis:

- Right-click the Y-axis.

- Choose **Format Axis**.

- Under the **Scale** tab, input the minimum and maximum values that you want to use and deselect the corresponding *Auto* check boxes.

- Click **OK**.

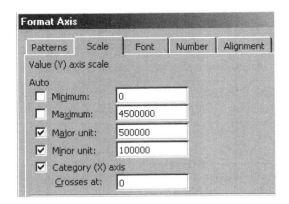

Changing the units used in the Y-axis

To change the units used in the Y-axis:

- Right-click the Y-axis.

- Choose **Format Axis**.

- Under the **Scale** tab, in the *Display units* section, click the arrow to the right of the *Display units* drop-down list.

- Select a value of your choice.

- Click **OK**.

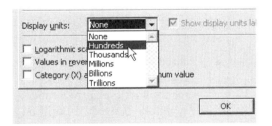

Changing the intervals used in the Y-axis

To change the intervals used in the Y-axis:

- Right-click the Y-axis.

- Choose **Format Axis**.

- Under the **Scale** tab, input the major unit and minor unit values that you want to use, and deselect the corresponding *Auto* check boxes.

- Click **OK**.

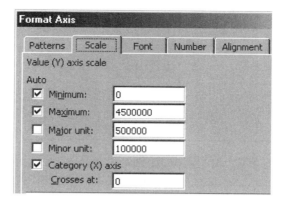

Pie charts

You will recall that pie charts represent the parts of a whole as segments of a circle. Note that if the numbers represented by the pie segments are percentages, then they *must* add up to 100. Otherwise, you will create a false impression.

In PowerPoint you can create different types of pie charts, from simple 2-D pie charts to exploded 3-D pie charts. An exploded pie chart is a chart in which one or more of the segments are separated from the others. You can rotate and change the elevation of these slices for greater emphasis, and you can label them to ensure that your audience can interpret the pie chart fully. For example, you can rotate the pie to bring a particular segment to the top. Take a look at the following exercise, where you rotate and change the elevation of an exploded pie chart.

Exercise 5.4: Adding 3-D effects to an exploded pie chart

1) Open EX5.4.PPT. Go to slide number 15, 'Best Sellers'.

2) Double-click the pie chart so that the datasheet appears.

3) Right-click the chart area and choose the **3-D View** option from the menu.

4) In the *3-D View* dialog box, change the elevation of the pie chart to 45 degrees. You can do this in one of two ways:

   ■ Click the **Up** and **Down** arrow buttons until the Elevation box reads 45.

   -or-

■ Input the number 45 directly into the *Elevation* box.

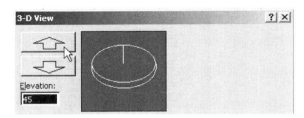

5) In the *3-D View* dialog box, change the rotation of the pie chart to 40°. You can do this in one of two ways:

■ Click the **Left** and **Right** rotation arrow buttons until the *Rotation* box reads 40.

-or-

■ Input the number 40 directly into the *Rotation* box.

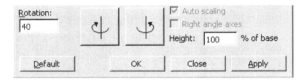

Click **Apply**, then click **OK**.

Your pie chart should look as shown.

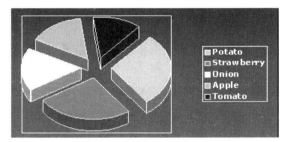

Well done! You have changed both the rotation and elevation of the pie chart.

Now add labels to the different pie segments.

Exercise 5.5: Adding labels to pie segments

1) Open EX5.5.PPT. Go to slide number 15, 'Best Sellers'.

2) Double-click the pie chart so that the datasheet appears.

3) Right-click the pie chart and choose **Format Data Series** from the menu that appears.

4) Under the **Data Labels** tab in the *Format Data Series* dialog box, select the *Show percent* option.

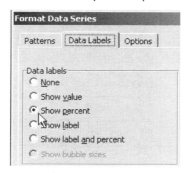

Click **OK**.

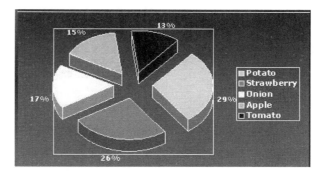

Your pie chart should look as shown.

Chapter 5: summary

You can import information such as a *cell range* from an Excel spreadsheet into PowerPoint. You can use this *quantitative information* to form the basis of a chart. There are several *chart types* to choose from: *bar charts*, *column charts*, *line charts* and *pie charts*. You can mix chart types together to form *combination charts*. A combination chart is used to show the relationship between different *kinds* of information. You can adjust your combination chart in various ways – you can change the *scale* of the *Y-axis* (value axis), change the types of units used on it, and change its intervals.

Pie charts represent the parts of a whole as segments of a circle. You can adjust a *3-D* pie chart by changing the degrees of *elevation* and *rotation* in the chart. And you can *label* the data slices in your pie chart.

Chapter 5: quick quiz

Circle the correct answer to each of the following questions about charts.

Q1	What's the best chart type to use for comparing quantities, such as sales figures?
A.	Bar chart.
B.	Line chart.
C.	Column chart.
D.	Pie chart.

Q2	To change the intervals used in the Y-axis you …
A.	Right-click the Y-axis and choose **Format Axis**. Under the **Scale** tab click the arrow to the right of the *Display units* box. Select the values required and click **OK**.
B.	Right-click the Y-axis and choose **Format Axis**. Under the **Scale** tab input the major and minor unit values and deselect the corresponding *Auto* values. Click **OK**.
C.	Right-click the Y-axis and choose **Format Axis**. Under the **Scale** tab input the minimum and maximum values and deselect the corresponding *Auto* values. Click **OK**.
D.	Right-click the Y-axis and choose **Format Axis**. Under the **Number** tab click the arrow to the right of the *Display units* box. Select 1000s and click **OK**.

Q3	True or false – you can create 3-D combination charts.
A.	True.
B.	False.

Q4	To format a chart you ...
A.	Right-click the chart and select **Clear**. Input the *Patterns* options and then input the *Marker* options.
B.	Right-click the chart and select **Add Treadline**. Input the *Patterns* options and then input the *Marker* options. Click **OK**.
C.	Right-click the chart and select **Chart Type**. Input the *Patterns* options and then input the *Marker* options. Click **OK**.
D.	Right-click the chart and select **Format Data Series**. Input the *Patterns* options and then input the *Marker* options. Click **OK**.

Answers

1: C, **2:** B, **3:** B, **4:** D.

6

Action buttons and hyperlinks

In this chapter you will learn how to create action buttons and hyperlinks in order to navigate through your presentation, and from it to other information resources. You route these hyperlinks and action buttons to specific locations such as individual slides, other presentations, websites, Word documents, and so on.

In this chapter you will also learn how to use the comment box, which is the PowerPoint equivalent of a 'sticky note'.

New skills

At the end of this chapter you should be able to:

- Place action buttons
- Format action buttons
- Place hyperlinks
- Reroute action buttons
- Reroute hyperlinks
- Insert comments
- Adjust comments
- Remove comments

New words

At the end of this chapter you should be able to explain the following terms:

- Action button
- Hyperlink
- Comment box

This chapter covers the following syllabus points:

- AM 6.6.1.1
- AM 6.6.1.2

Action buttons

A PowerPoint action button is an AutoShape that you place in a presentation to help you navigate through the slide show. Action buttons are especially useful when you want to go directly from one slide to another specific slide. If you want an action button to appear on every slide in a presentation you place it on the slide master. If you want an action button to appear on certain slides, then you place the button on those slides only. Look at the following exercise for an example of how to create and place an action button that will appear throughout a presentation.

Exercise 6.1: Creating and placing action buttons

1) Open EX6.1.PPT. Go to the Slide Master – **View | Master | Slide Master**.

2) Choose **AutoShapes | Action Buttons** from the *Drawing* toolbar and then select the **Home** action button.

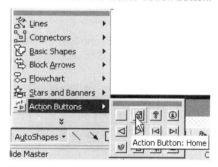

3) Place your cursor anywhere on the Master page; it turns into crosshairs. Drag the crosshairs to draw a **Home** button.

4) The *Action Settings* dialog box appears. Under the **Mouse Click** tab, select the *Hyperlink to* option. Choose *Next Slide* from the drop-down list.

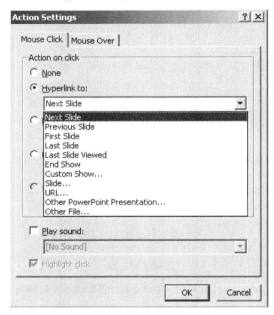

Click **OK**.

5) To adjust the colour of the action button, right-click it and choose **Format AutoShape** from the menu.

6) Under the **Colors and Lines** tab of the *Format AutoShape* dialog box, click the arrow to the right of the *Color* box. Select a light purple colour. (This colour is part of your colour scheme.)

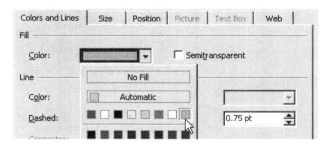

Click **OK**.

7) Use the arrow keys to move the action button to the bottom-right of the slide master (the number area). Resize the action button to fit the number area box.

Your slide master should look as shown.

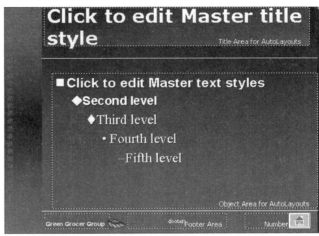

Assigning action buttons to other locations

You can assign action buttons to the following locations: websites, files, slides or other slide shows.

Assign an action button to a website

Start as in Exercise 6.1. In the **Mouse Click** tab of the *Action Settings* dialog box:

■ Select the *Hyperlink to* option.

■ Click the arrow to the right of the *Hyperlink to* box.

■ Select *URL* from the list.

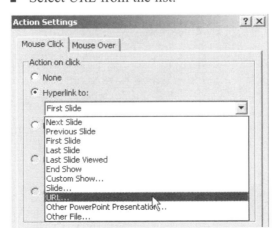

- Type the url you need in the *Hyperlink To URL* dialog box and click **OK**.

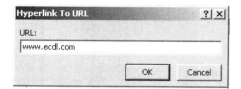

- Click **OK**.

Assign an action button to a file

Start as in Exercise 6.1. In the **Mouse Click** tab of the *Action Settings* dialog box:

- Select the *Hyperlink to* option.
- Click the arrow to the right of the *Hyperlink to* box.
- Select *Other File* from the list.

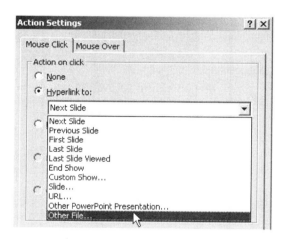

- Navigate to the file that you want and click **OK**.
- Click **OK**.

Assign an action button to a slide

Start as in Exercise 6.1. In the **Mouse Click** tab of the *Action Settings* dialog box:

- Select the *Hyperlink to* option.
- Click the arrow to the right of the *Hyperlink to* box.
- Select *Slide* from the list.

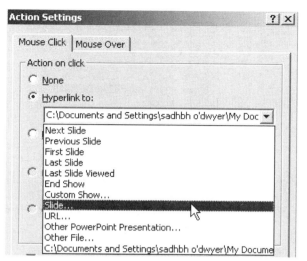

- Select the slide that you want from the *Hyperlink To Slide* dialog box and click **OK**.

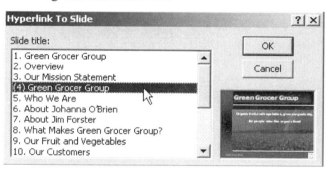

- Click **OK**.

Assign an action button to another slide show

Start as in Exercise 6.1. In the **Mouse Click** tab of the *Action Settings* dialog box:

- Click the arrow to the right of the *Hyperlink to* box.

- Select *Other PowerPoint Presentation* from the list.

- Navigate to the slide show that you want from the *Hyperlink to Other PowerPoint Presentation* dialog box and click **OK**.

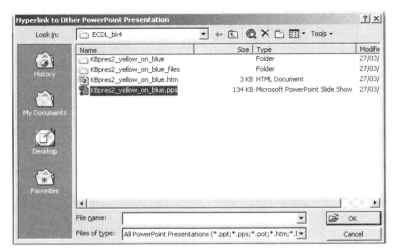

- In the *Hyperlink To Slide* dialog box select the slide that you want to display first, and click **OK**.

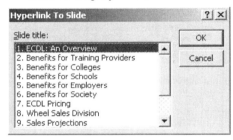

- Click **OK**.

Rerouting action buttons

If you create an action button but then decide to change its destination you can reroute it to an alternative location. When you set up the action button in Exercise 6.1, you assigned it to the *Next Slide* option. In the exercise below you will reroute this action button to the first slide of the presentation.

Exercise 6.2: Rerouting an action button

1) Open EX6.2.PPT. Choose **View | Master | Slide Master**.

2) Right-click the action button on the slide master. Choose **Action Settings** from the menu.

3) Under the **Mouse Click** tab, click the *Hyperlink to* option. Select *First Slide* from the drop-down list.

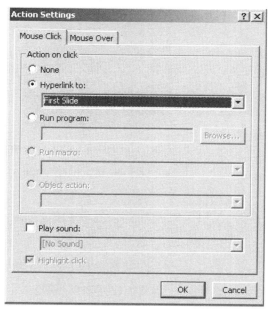

4) Click **OK**.

5) Go to Slide Show view and check that, from any slide, the action button brings you to the first slide.

Hyperlinks

Like action buttons, pieces of text, graphics or shapes can be hyperlinked to other locations: websites, slides, presentations or files. Note that hyperlinks are not active while you are creating your presentation – they are active only in Slide Show view.

In the next exercise you will create a hyperlink from a piece of text in your presentation to an organic farming website.

Exercise 6.3: Inserting a hyperlink in a presentation

1) Open EX6.3.PPT. Select slide number 12, 'Organic Farming Practices'.

2) Select the item that you want to hyperlink from – you can choose a graphic, a shape or a piece of text. Here you will link from a piece of text, as shown below:

Hyperlink button

3) Place a hyperlink on the slide in one of following ways:

■ Click the hyperlink button on the *Standard* toolbar.

-or-

■ Choose **Insert | Hyperlink**.

-or-

■ Press the shortcut key **Ctrl+k**.

The *Insert Hyperlink* dialog box appears.

4) Click the **ScreenTip** button. In the *ScreenTip text* box type the following text:

European Organics

(This is the text that will appear when you place your cursor on the hyperlink.)

Click **OK** to close the *Set Hyperlink ScreenTip* dialog box.

5) In the *Type the file or Web page name* box, type the url of the website you want to link to:

http://www.organic-research.com

(If you don't know the name of the website, you can browse the Internet for it. Click the **Web Page** button to navigate to your chosen site. Copy and paste the url to the *Type the file or Web page name* box.)

Click **OK** to close the *Insert Hyperlink* box.

6) View your hyperlink in Slide Show view – press **F5**, or choose **View | Slide Show**, or click the **Slide Show** button.

7) Click the link to check that it works. Press **Esc** to return to the presentation.

Add a comment note

You can put the PowerPoint equivalent of a 'sticky note' on a slide. For example, if your presentation is being reviewed by other people, they might want to make a suggestion in a comment note. Or you might leave a comment note for yourself when you are working on a slide and you want to come back to it later.

Exercise 6.4: Adding a comment note to a slide

1) Open EX6.4.PPT. Go to slide number 12, 'Organic Farming Practices'.

2) Choose **Insert | Comment**. A yellow 'sticky note' appears in the left corner of the slide showing your name (or the name of the person who registered the application).

3) Type the following text in the comment box:

> www.organic-europe.net — more up-to-date information?

```
Denis O'Dwyer:
www.organic-
europe.net --
more up-to-date
information?
```

Assigning hyperlinks

In the previous exercise you created a hyperlink to a website. However, you can also assign hyperlinks to other locations: slides, files or other presentations.

Assigning a hyperlink to a slide

Place in This Document button

To assign a hyperlink to a slide you:

- Click the **Insert Hyperlink** button.

- In the *Insert Hyperlink* dialog box, click the **Place in This Document** button.

- In the *Select a place in this document* box, select the slide that you want to link to. (If necessary, click the + box, to see a full list of slide titles.)

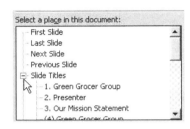

- Click **OK**.

Assigning a hyperlink to a file or another presentation

Existing File or Web Page button

To assign a hyperlink to a file or presentation you:

- Click the **Insert Hyperlink** button.

- In the *Insert Hyperlink* dialog box, click the **Existing File or Web Page** button.

- Click the **File** button in the *Browse for* section.

- In the *Link to File* dialog box, navigate to the file or presentation that you want and click **OK**.

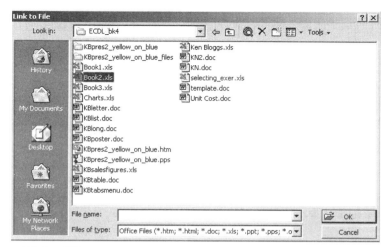

■ Click **OK**.

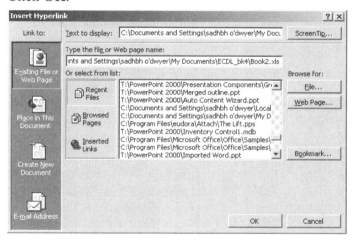

Rerouting hyperlinks

Just as you can reroute an action button, you can also reroute a hyperlink to another location.

Exercise 6.5: Rerouting a hyperlink

1) Open EX6.5.PPT. Go to slide number 12, 'Organic Farming Practices'. (This is the slide on which you put a comment note.)

2) Right-click the *Organic Farming in Europe* hyperlink. Choose **Hyperlink | Edit Hyperlink** from the menu.

The *Edit Hyperlink* dialog box appears.

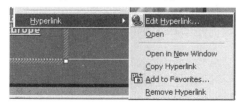

3) Copy the url of the website (www.organic-europe.net) from the comment note to the *Type the file or Web page name* box. Click **OK**.

4) Remove the comment note – select the comment note and press **Delete**.

5) View your hyperlink in Slide Show view – press **F5**, or choose **View | Slide Show**, or click the **Slide Show** button. Check to see that the hyperlink works.

Chapter 6: summary

Action buttons are AutoShapes that help you to navigate within your slide show or from your slide show to another location. You can edit an action button or *reroute* it to another location. *Hyperlinks* link items such as text, graphics or shapes in your presentation to other locations. You can also *reroute* a hyperlink to other locations such as websites, presentations or files. The *comment note* works like a 'sticky note'. Insert a comment note to add suggestions or references to slides while you are still developing your presentation.

Chapter 6: quick quiz

Circle the correct answer to each of the following questions about action buttons and hyperlinks.

Q1	To reassign an action button to an alternative location you …
A.	Right-click and choose **Format AutoShape**. Under the **Mouse Click** tab, click the *Hyperlink to* option. Select the alternative location from the drop-down list. Click **OK**.
B.	Right-click and choose **Action Settings**. Under the **Mouse Over** tab, click the *Hyperlink to* option. Select the alternative location from the drop-down list. Click **OK**.
C.	Right-click and choose **Format AutoShape**. Under the **Mouse Over** tab, click the *Hyperlink to* option. Select the alternative location from the drop-down list. Click **OK**.
D.	Right-click and choose **Action Settings**. Under the **Mouse Click** tab, click the *Hyperlink to* option. Select the alternative location from the drop-down list. Click **OK**.

Q2	To assign a hyperlink to a slide in your presentation, you click ...
A.	**Insert Hyperlink**. Insert the url of the hyperlink and then click the **Existing File or Web Page** button. Select the slide you want to use in the *Insert Hyperlink* dialog box. Click **OK**.
B.	**Insert Hyperlink**. Insert the url of the hyperlink and then click the **E-mail Address** button. Select the slide you want to use in the *Insert Hyperlink* dialog box. Click **OK**.
C.	**Insert Hyperlink**. Insert the url of the hyperlink and then click the **Place in This Document** button. Select the slide you want to use in the *Insert Hyperlink* dialog box. Click **OK**.
D.	**Insert Hyperlink**. Insert the url of the hyperlink and then click the **Create New Document** button. Select the slide you want to use in the *Insert Hyperlink* dialog box. Click **OK**.

Q3	The shortcut key to insert a hyperlink is ...
A.	**Ctrl+h**.
B.	**Ctrl+k**.
C.	**Ctrl+f**.
D.	**Ctrl+p**.

Q4	To reroute a hyperlink you ...
A.	Right-click the hyperlink and select **Remove Hyperlink**. Type the url in the *Type the file or Web page name* box. Click **OK**.
B.	Right-click the hyperlink and select **Edit Hyperlink**. Type the url in the *Type the file or Web page name* box. Click **OK**.
C.	Right-click the hyperlink and select **Copy Hyperlink**. Type the url in the *Type the file or Web page name* box. Click **OK**.
D.	Right-click the hyperlink and select **Edit Hyperlink**. Type the url in the *Type the file or Web page name* box.

Q5	True or false – a comment can be seen in Slide Show view.
A.	True.
B.	False.

Answers

1: D, **2:** C, **3:** B, **4:** B, **5:** A.

7

Custom shows and slide shows

In this chapter

Usually, a presentation will follow a linear path from the first slide to the last. However, details of financial performance might not be of relevance to farmers, for example, and details of crop performance might not be of interest to financiers. PowerPoint enables us to produce custom shows, where you specify different paths through the slides, each path containing a different subset of the slides. In this chapter you will specify two custom shows within your presentation.

Also in this chapter, when you save your presentation, you can save it as a slide show and you can adapt the slide show to suit the particular location and audience.

New skills

At the end of this chapter you should be able to:

- Create a custom show
- Run a custom show
- Edit a custom show
- Create a summary slide for custom shows
- Create a slide show
- Set up slide shows for different audience types

New words

At the end of this chapter you should be able to explain the following terms:

- Custom show
- Summary slide
- Slide show set ups

Syllabus reference	This chapter covers the following syllabus points:

- AM 6.6.1.4
- AM 6.6.2.1
- AM 6.6.2.2
- AM 6.6.2.3

Custom shows

If you are presenting at different times to different groups of people, your presentation is likely to contain some slides that are particularly relevant to a particular audience, and other slides that are of no relevance to them whatsoever. By creating custom shows, you can present a selected group of slides from your presentation, in a particular order, to each different audience.

> **Custom show**
>
> *A custom show is a subset of slides from within a presentation, designed to appeal to a specific audience.*

Creating a custom show

Before you create your custom show, you must decide what slides you wish to work with. There are two different audiences for the Green Grocer presentation:

- Suppliers to the Green Grocer Group.
- Investors in the Green Grocer Group.

Each group has a common interest in the Green Grocer Group, but each requires different levels of detail about different topics. Therefore, you will create a custom show with slides on organic practice and another custom show with slides on financial performance.

Here's how you do it.

Exercise 7.1: Creating custom shows
1) Open EX7.1.PPT.

2) Choose **Slide Show | Custom Shows**. The *Custom Shows* dialog box appears.

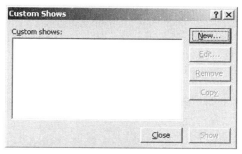

3) Click **New**. The *Define Custom Show* dialog box appears.

4) In the *Slide show name* box, give your custom show a name:

   `Organic Practice`

5) From the list of slides shown in the *Slides in presentation* box, select in turn each slide you want to include in the custom show and click the **Add>>** button. This moves them to the *Slides in custom show* box. Select slides 9, 10, 11, 12 and 13.

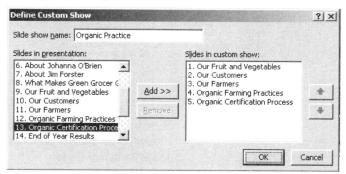

   Click **OK**.

6) Create a second custom show in exactly the same way, called 'Financial Growth', and including slides 14 to 17.

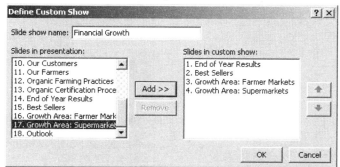

   At any time, you can view a custom show by choosing **Slide Show | Custom Shows**, selecting the custom show and clicking **Show**.

Editing your custom shows

Now that you have created a custom show, you can return to it and edit it to suit you. You can reorder the slides, include more slides, or remove slides you previously used. The next exercise will show you how.

Exercise 7.2: Editing your custom shows

1) Open EX7.2.PPT.

2) Choose **Slide Show** | **Custom Shows** and select the Organic Practice custom show.

   Click the **Edit** button.

3) Rearrange the order of the custom show slides. Select slide 5, 'Organic Certification Process', and click the **Up** button to move it to the top of the list. Click **OK**.

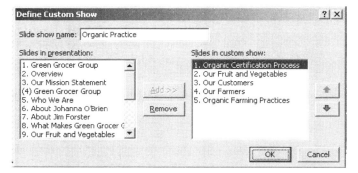

4) Select the 'Financial Growth' custom show and click the **Edit** button.

5) Rearrange the order of the custom show slides. Select slide 3, 'Growth Area: Farmer Markets', and click the **Down** button to move it to the bottom of the list.

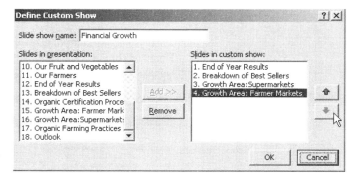

   Click **OK**.

6) Select each custom show in turn, and click **Show** to view them.

Summary slides

Summary slides are especially useful when you have custom shows in your presentation. A summary slide is like a table of contents, in that it contains slide titles. A summary slide is often used as a 'launchpad' for custom shows. You include the custom show slide titles on a summary slide, and then hyperlink from them to the custom shows.

> **Summary slide**
>
> *A summary slide gives the table of contents of a presentation. It usually contains hyperlinks to custom shows.*

The following exercise shows you how to create a summary slide.

Exercise 7.3: Creating a summary slide

1) Open EX7.3.PPT.

2) Choose **View | Slide Sorter**.

3) Select all the slides whose titles you want to appear on the summary slide. In this case, select the first slide of each of the two custom shows you've created: slides 13 and 14. (Click **Ctrl** and select them in turn.)

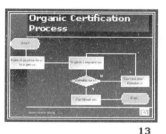
13

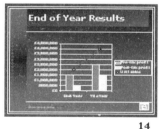
14

4) Click the **Summary Slide** button on the *Slide Sorter* toolbar.

A new slide appears as number 13, 'Summary Slide'.

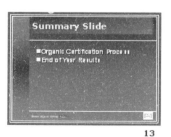
13

14

*Summary
Slide
button*

Notice that it contains the title of the first slide in each of your custom shows – 'Organic Certification Process' and 'End of Year Results'.

5) Let's change the position of the summary slide. Drag the summary slide from slide 13 to the position of slide 3.

2

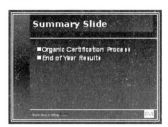

3

6) Edit your summary slide by double-clicking it:

- Change the title of the slide to the following:

  Overview

- Type the following text before the first bullet point:

  In this presentation we will focus on:

- Add the text (of interest to growers) to 'Organic Certification Process'

- Add the text (of interest to financiers) to 'End of Year Results'

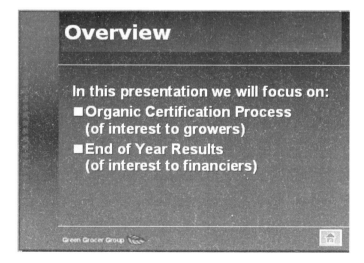

Activating your summary slide

Your summary slide contains your custom show names. Now you must activate them, so that you can navigate to the custom shows from the summary slide. You do this by assigning a hyperlink to each of the titles on the summary slide. The following exercise will show you how to do this.

Exercise 7.4: Accessing custom shows from the summary slide

1) Open EX7.4.PPT. Go to slide 3, 'Overview'.

2) Select the second bullet point 'End of Year Results'.

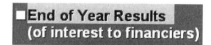

Insert Hyperlink button

3) Click the **Insert Hyperlink** button.

4) In the *Insert Hyperlink* dialog box, click the **Place in This Document** button.

5) In the *Select a place in this document* box, select the 'Financial Growth' custom show.

6) Select the *Show and return* check box. Click **OK**.

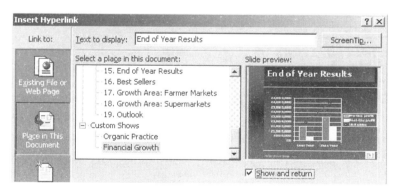

7) Repeat steps 2–6 to link the Organic Certification Process title to the Organic Practice custom show.

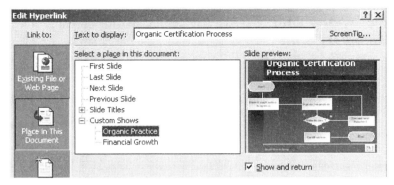

Your summary slide should now look as shown.

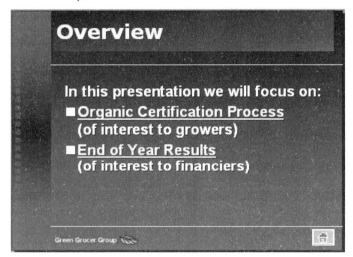

Well done! You can now access your custom shows directly from the summary slide.

Different types of slide shows

The most obvious use of a presentation is as a slide show supporting a presenter with an audience in a conference room. This requires that the audience be in the same place at the same time as the presenter, who controls the delivery of the presentation. However, there are other ways of using PowerPoint presentations. For example:

- Self-running slide show for website use – such as a company intranet.

- Self-running slide show for use in a kiosk – such as in a trade show.

- Slide show with limited viewer control – such as sharing on a computer network.

To choose one of these options, you first save your presentation as a slide show. (A slide show has the ending .PPS, but unlike a presentation PPT file, a PPS file will automatically open in Slide Show view.)

Exercise 7.5: Save a presentation as a slide show

1) Open EX7.5.PPT.

2) Choose **File | Save As**.

3) Ensure the following appears in the *File name* box:

   EX7.5

4) Click the arrow to the right of the *Save as type* box and select *PowerPoint Show (*.pps)*.

   Click the **Save** button.

   You now have a slide show called EX7.5.PPS.

Setting up slide shows

You can create different slide show setups by using the **Set Up Show** command. For example, in the following exercise you will set up a self-running slide show to run on the company network. You will not be present at the slide show, but the viewer will work through the slides by herself.

Exercise 7.6: Set up a self-running slide show

1) Open EX7.6.PPT.

2) Choose **Slide Show | Set Up Show**. The *Set Up Show* dialog box appears.

3) Under *Show type* select:

   - *Browsed by an individual (window)*.

   - *Loop continuously until 'Esc'*.

   - *Show scrollbar*.

4) Under *Slides*, select *All*.

5) Under *Advance slides*, select *Manually*.

6) Click **OK**.

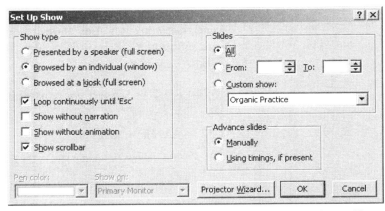

7) Press **F5** to see how your slide show will appear to the viewer. The viewer can navigate through the slides in different ways:

- **Page Up** and **Page Down** keys.

- **Forward** and **Back** buttons on the *Web* toolbar.

- Choosing **Browse | Advance** or **Reverse** on the menu bar.

Chapter 7: summary

PowerPoint enables us to produce *custom shows*. A *custom show* is like a presentation within a presentation; you specify different paths through the presentation slides and each path contains a different subset of the slides.

A summary slide is like the table of contents of your presentation, and you can use it to place hyperlinks to custom shows.

You can *set up* your slide show in different ways. For example, you can set up a self-running presentation that can be viewed at a kiosk in a trade show, or set up a slide show that can be viewed over your company network.

Chapter 7: quick quiz

Circle the correct answer to each of the following questions about shows.

Q1	To view a custom show you ...
A.	Choose **Slide Show | View Show**. Select the custom show that you want to view and click **Show**.
B.	Choose **Slide Show | Custom Shows**. Select the custom show that you want to view and click **Edit**.
C.	Choose **Slide Show | Custom Shows**. Select the custom show that you want to view and click **Show**.
D.	Choose **Slide Show | Set Up Show**. Select the custom show that you want to view and click **OK**.

Q2	A self-running slide show ends in …
A.	.PPA.
B.	.POT.
C.	.PPT.
D.	.PPS.

Q3	In which view do you create a summary slide?
A.	Normal view
B.	Slide Sorter view.
C.	Outline view.
D.	Slides view.

Q4	To set up a slide show to run continuously you …
A.	Choose **View	Slide Sorter**. Click the **Summary Slide** button and select the option *Loop Continuously until 'Esc'*. Click **OK**.
B.	Choose **Slide Show	Set Up Show**. Click **OK**.
C.	Choose **Slide Show	View Show**. Select the option *Loop Continuously until 'Esc'*. Click **OK**.
D.	Choose **Slide Show	Set Up Show**. Select the option *Loop Continuously until 'Esc'*. Click **OK**.

Answers　　　　**1:** C, **2:** D, **3:** B, **4:** D.

Transitions

In this chapter you will learn about transitions, and about the different ways of timing and advancing the slides in your presentation. Transitions add visual interest to your slide. You can advance slides manually or automatically. If your presentation is well scripted and rehearsed, or it is running independently, in a kiosk for example, you are likely to choose automatic advance; if you expect interaction with your audience, you are likely to choose manual advance.

If you choose automatic advance, PowerPoint enables you to fine-tune your timings while rehearsing your presentation.

New skills

At the end of this chapter you should be able to:

- Apply transition effects

- Apply transition timings

- Apply manual advance to slides

- Apply automatic advance to slides

- Rehearse and adjust automatic advance timings

- Switch between automatic and manual advance

New words

At the end of this chapter you should be able to explain the following terms:

- Transitions

- Slide advancing

- Rehearse timings

This chapter covers the following syllabus points:

- AM 6.6.1.3
- AM 6.6.1.5

Transition effects

A transition is the way in which a slide first appears in a slide show. A slide can 'dissolve' into another slide, for example, or 'wipe' across the screen – PowerPoint offers 42 different transition effects. These special effects help to keep your audience interested.

In this chapter you will apply transition effects to your presentation and vary the speed of the transitions. One word of warning, however: transitions should not take away from the content of your presentation. If you use too many different transition effects, your audience will be distracted. Therefore, don't use more than two or three: consistently using a small number of transition effects will add strength to your presentation.

Transition

A transition is the way in which a slide first appears in a PowerPoint slide show.

Choosing transitions

Think about your choice of transitions carefully. A good way to familiarize yourself with the transitions available is to apply the *Random Transition* effect to your presentation. In Slide Show view you can then see the different transitions at work and you can pick the ones that you want. Note that *Random Transition* uses all the available transition effects and is not suitable for presenting to an audience.

Exercise 8.1: Applying the random transition effect

1) Open EX8.1.PPT.

2) Choose **Slide Show | Slide Transition**.

3) Click the arrow to the right of the *Effect* box, and select the *Random Transition* effect.

4) Select a transition speed of *Fast*.

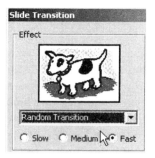

5) Select the *On mouse click* check box to advance the transitions manually.

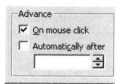

6) Click the **Apply to All** button to apply the *Random Transition* effect to all the slides in the presentation.

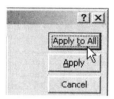

You've now applied the *Random Transition* effect to your presentation. Press **F5** to see how the various transition effects look during a presentation. When you've finished viewing, you can then choose the transition effects that are most suitable.

Applying transitions

In the previous exercise, you saw the range of available transition effects. The ones that you will use in these exercises are:

- *Box Out*
- *Dissolve*
- *Wipe Down*

Use the *Box Out* option for the majority of the slides in the slide show and keep the *Dissolve* and *Wipe Down* options for emphasizing special points.

Exercise 8.2: Applying selected transition effects

1) Open EX8.2.PPT.

2) Choose **Slide Show | Slide Transition**.

3) Click the arrow to the right of the *Effect* box and select the *Box Out* effect.

4) Select a transition speed of *Medium*.

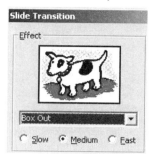

5) Select the *On mouse click* check box to advance the transitions manually.

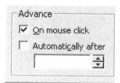

6) Click the **Apply to All** button to apply the *Box Out* effect to all the slides in the presentation.

7) In the Outline pane, select slide 15, 'End of Year Results', and slide 16, 'Best Sellers'.

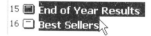

8) Choose **Slide Show | Slide Transition**. Click the arrow to the right of the *Effect* box and select the *Dissolve* effect.

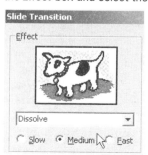

9) Click the **Apply** button.

10) In the Outline pane, select slide 1, 'Green Grocer Group'.

1 ☐ **Green Grocer Group**

11) Choose **Slide Show | Slide Transition**. Click the arrow to the right of the *Effect* box and select the *Wipe Down* option.

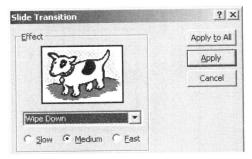

12) Click the **Apply** button.

Congratulations! You've applied the *Box Out* transition effect to the majority of the slides in the presentation. And, for greater emphasis, you've added the *Dissolve* effect to two slides in the presentation, and the *Wipe Down* effect to the title slide. Look at your presentation in Slide Show view and view your progress.

Transition timings

Transition effects can be run at three different speeds: fast, medium and slow.

In the next exercise you will edit the timings of your transitions.

Exercise 8.3: Editing transition timings

1) Open EX8.3.PPT.

2) Go to slide 2, 'Presenter'.

3) Choose **Slide Show | Slide Transition**.

4) In the *Slide Transition* dialog box, select a transition speed of *Slow*.

5) Click the **Apply** button.

6) View your presentation in Slide Show view. Note the difference between the transition to the second slide and the following transitions.

Advancing slides

How do you want to advance the slides in your slide show? Would you prefer to do this manually or automatically? Before you make a decision, let's see what's involved.

Manual advance

If your presentation entails a lot of audience participation, you must choose manual advance, as you can't predict the length of time you will spend on each slide.

You advance slides by clicking the mouse or by using any of the following short-cut keys:

- Next slide   **Page Down** button
- Previous slide   **Page Up** button
- First slide   **Home** button
- Last slide   **End** button

A disadvantage of using manual advance is that you might block the view of your audience when you lean over to click the mouse or use the short-cut keys. You could solve this problem by using a wireless mouse – this would enable you to walk around the room while advancing the slides.

Automatic advance

If you can predict the length of time you will spend on each slide or if the slide show will run unattended, you will choose automatic advance. However, some people are uncomfortable with automatic advance settings, as they feel restricted by them. If this is the case, you can remove the automatic advance settings and revert to manual advance.

Exercise 8.4: Setting up automatic advance

1) Open EX8.4.PPT.

2) Choose **Slide Show | Slide Transition**.

3) Under *Advance*, select the *Automatically after* check box.

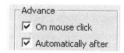

4) Input an advance time of 15 seconds.

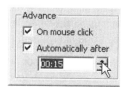

5) Click the **Apply to All** button to apply the changes to all the slides in the presentation.

Press **F5** to view the automatic advance timing.

Note: If both the *On mouse click* and *Automatically after* check boxes are selected, the next slide will appear *either* when the mouse is clicked *or* after the advance time specified, depending on which comes first.

Rehearse timings

Every presentation benefits from rehearsal. Rehearsal is especially necessary if you have set up automatic timings for your slides. You can rehearse timings with the *Rehearse Timings* feature, which enables you to test the automatic timings you have allotted to your slides. You might find that some slides require less or more time than you have allowed.

Let's explore the *Rehearse Timings* feature and see if some of the slides in the presentation could benefit from a timing change.

Rehearse Timings
If you choose automatic advance, Rehearse Timings enables you to run through your slide show in real time to check that the timings fit your presentation, and to fine-tune them, if necessary.

Exercise 8.5: Using the rehearse timings option
1) Open EX8.5.PPT.

2) Choose **View | Slide Sorter**.

Rehearse Timings button

3) Click the **Rehearse Timings** button on the *Slide Sorter* toolbar.

PowerPoint launches into Slide Show view with the *Rehearsal* dialog box in the top left corner of the slide.

4) Deliver your presentation as if you were in front of your audience, but advancing from slide to slide using one of the manual methods. (If this is a self-running presentation, check that the viewer will have enough time to absorb the information on each slide.)

5) When you have finished your delivery, click the **Close** button in the top-right corner of the *Rehearsal* dialog box.

6) While you were rehearsing, PowerPoint recorded the time that you spent on each slide. It now asks if you want to keep the new timing: press **Yes**. The timing allocated to each slide now matches your actual delivery speed precisely.

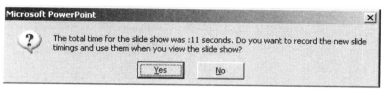

Removing the automatic advance timings

You can easily remove the automatic advance timings and revert to manual advance. You will see this in the following exercise.

Exercise 8.6: Remove automatic advance timing

1) Open EX8.6.PPT.

2) Go to slide 1, 'Green Grocer Group'.

3) Choose **Slide Show | Slide Transition**.

4) In the *Advance* section of the *Slide Transition* dialog box deselect the *Automatically after* check box.

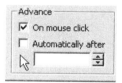

Leave the *On mouse click* check box selected.

5) Click the **Apply** button.

6) Press **F5** to view your presentation in Slide Show view.

Chapter 8: summary

A *transition* is the way in which a slide first appears in a slide show. Slide transitions are useful as they help to keep your audience interested. PowerPoint offers a wide range of transition effects, such as *Box Out* and *Dissolve*.

Advancing from one slide to the next can be done either *manually* or *automatically*. If you use automatic advance, you need to decide on the length of time each slide is displayed. PowerPoint refers to this as slide *timings*.

You can *rehearse* and *adjust* your slide timings with the *Rehearse Timings* option. If you want, you can remove the automatic timings and revert to manual advance.

Circle the correct answer to each of the following questions about transitions.

Q1	Find the example of a transition effect from the list below.
A.	Disappear.
B.	Charcoal.
C.	Wipers.
D.	Box out.

Q2	For manual advance, which shortcut key do you use to go to the previous slide in a presentation?
A.	**Page Up**.
B.	**Page Down**.
C.	**Ctrl**.
D.	**Space bar**.

Q3	How do you rehearse the timings of your slide show?
A.	Choose **View | Normal**. Click the **Rehearse Timings** button and deliver your presentation as if you were in front of the audience. Advance the slides manually.
B.	Choose **Slide Show | Set Up Show**. Click the **Rehearse Timings** button and deliver your presentation as if you were in front of the audience. Advance the slides automatically.
C.	Choose **View | Slide Sorter**. Click the **Rehearse Timings** button and deliver your presentation as if you were in front of the audience. Advance the slides manually.
D.	Choose **Slide Show | Slide Transition**. Click the **Rehearse Timings** button and deliver your presentation as if you were in front of the audience. Advance the slides automatically.

Q4	How do you remove automatic advance timings for all slides?
A.	Choose **Slide Show | Slide Transition**. Deselect the *Automatically after* check box and select **Apply to All**.
B.	Choose **Slide Show | Slide Transition**. Deselect the *Automatically after* check box and select **Apply**.
C.	Choose **View | Slide Sorter**. Click the **Rehearse Timings** button and press **Close**.
D.	Choose **View | Master | Slide Master**. Click the **Slide Transition** button and deselect the *Automatically after* check box and select **Apply to All**.

Q5	True or false – a PowerPoint slide show will not work if you select both the manual advance and the automatic advance options.
A.	True.
B.	False.

Answers

1: D, **2:** B, **3:** C, **4:** A, **5:** B.

Animation effects

In this chapter

You can apply animation to each element in a slide (text, graphics, drawn objects). When you do, the elements will appear in a sequence and in a manner that you specify.

In this chapter you will explore animations in depth. You will edit existing animations and apply animation techniques to text and charts. You'll take your animation skills further by working with multimedia tools, such as audio effects and movies. Let your own creativity take over!

New skills

At the end of this chapter you should be able to:

- Change the order in which elements appear on a slide
- Edit animation timings
- Add animation to text
- Add animation to charts
- Insert audio effects
- Insert movies
- Identify audio and movie file types

New words

At the end of this chapter you should be able to explain the following terms:

- Animation order sequence
- Dimming

This chapter covers the following syllabus points:

- AM 6.5.1.1
- AM 6.5.1.2
- AM 6.5.2.1
- AM 6.5.2.2
- AM 6.5.2.3
- AM 6.5.2.4

Editing your animations

Animations are very flexible. You can change the following:

- The sequence in which the elements appear.
- The manner in which each element appears.
- The advance method used to reveal each element.

Exercise 9.1: Editing order and timings of an animation

1) Open EX9.1.PPT.

2) Go to slide number 10, 'Our Fruit and Vegetables'.

3) Choose **Slide Show | Custom Animation**.

   Note that the following check boxes have been selected in the *Check to animate slide objects* section:

   - Picture frame 4
   - Picture frame 5
   - Picture frame 6

4) Click the **Preview** button to see the order in which the animated elements appear.

5) Select the **Order & Timing** tab of the *Custom Animation* dialog box.

6) Select *Picture frame 6* in the *Animation order* box, and click the **Move Up** button to send it to the middle of the animation sequence.

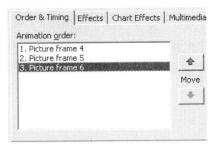

The animation sequence should now look as shown.

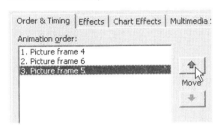

7) In the *Start animation* section, select *On mouse click*. Each element will now appear in sequence when you click the mouse. (If you want elements to appear with automatic timing, select *Automatically* and input a number of seconds in the *Automatically* box.)

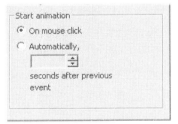

8) Click the **Preview** button to see the effect of your changes. If you are happy with your changes, press **OK**.

In Slide Show view, you can verify that clicking the mouse causes each element to appear in the sequence you specified.

Animation effects

You might think that the word animation refers to moving graphics only. In fact, you can in addition animate other elements, such as text and drawn objects. In addition PowerPoint animations can be used to add sound effects and dynamic changes of colour to elements on a slide.

A particularly useful animation effect is dimming, in which a piece of text or another slide element changes colour, or even disappears from the slide once it has been seen, or the next element is displayed.

> **Dimming**
>
> *Dimming is an animation effect that causes a slide element to change colour (typically to a lighter shade) or to disappear when the next element is introduced.*

Try the following exercise to see how effective text animation really is.

Exercise 9.2: Animating text

1) Open EX9.2.PPT.

2) Go to slide 12, 'Our Farmers'.

3) Choose **Slide Show | Custom Animation**.

4) In the *Check to animate slide objects* section, select the *Text 2* check box.

5) Select the **Effects** tab in the *Custom Animation* dialog box. Here you will add audio, movement and colour to your text.

6) Select the following options to add animation and audio effects.

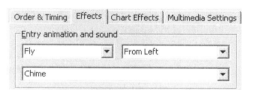

7) Select the following options to add motion.

(If you want, try out each of the motion effects: *All at once*, *By Word* and *By Letter*. Press **Preview** to see which effect you prefer.)

8) Now apply the dimming effect. Click the arrow to the right of the *After animation* box and select *More Colors*. This is where you choose the colour that your text will change to when the next element appears in the slide.

9) Click the **Standard** tab of the *Colors* dialog box. Select the bright yellow colour shown in the diagram and click **OK**.

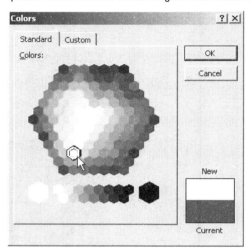

10) Click the **OK** button to close the *Custom Animation* dialog box.

11) View the slide in Slide Show view.

Exercise 9.3: Dimming drawn objects

1) Open EX9.2.PPT again, and go to slide 14, 'Organic Certification Process'.

2) View the slide in Slide Show view to see how animation has been applied to the groups of drawn objects in the slide.

3) Choose **Slide Show | Custom Animation**.

4) In the **Order and Timing** tab, select Group 8.

5) In the **Effects** tab, click the arrow to the right of the *After animation* box and select a light blue colour. Click **OK**.

6) View the slide again in Slide Show view. Notice that the group of objects you selected is dimmed when the next group is displayed.

Animating chart elements

PowerPoint enables you to animate charts, and thereby bring 'boring old numbers' to life. As with text and graphics, you can add motion, dynamic colour and audio effects to a chart. You can animate all the types of charts you saw in Chapter 5: pie charts, bar charts, line charts and so on.

Exercise 9.4: Animating chart elements

1) Open EX9.4.PPT. Go to slide 15, 'End of Year Results'.

2) Choose **Slide Show | Custom Animation**.

3) Select the *Chart 2* check box.

4) Select the **Chart Effects** tab.

5) Click the arrow to the right of the *Introduce chart elements* box. Select the *by Series* option and select the *Animate grid and legend* check box.

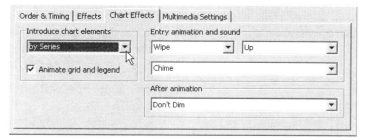

6) In the *Entry animation and sound* section, select the following:

- *Wipe*

- *Up*

- *Chime*

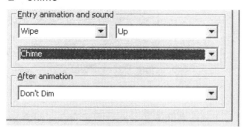

7) Click **OK**.

8) View your animated chart in Slide Show view. (Don't forget to turn on your speakers to hear the sound effects.)

In this exercise you animated the chart by series. However, depending on your chart type, you can choose other options in the *Introduce chart elements* box:

- *by Series* – this applies the animation effect in turn to each complete data series.

- *by Element in Series* – this applies the animation effect in turn to each data point in each data series.

- *by Category* – this applies the animation effect in turn to each complete grouping of data points on the Category axis.

- *by Element in Category* – this applies the animation effect in turn to each data point on the Category axis.

Try out the various options to see these animation effects at work. Note that some options are available only with certain chart types.

Audio effects

So far we have applied PowerPoint's pre-supplied audio effects, such as the *Chime* effect, to our animated slides. However, you can also use audio effects from other sources. You do this by:

- Inserting audio effects from PowerPoint's *Design Gallery Live*.

  -or-

- Recording your own audio effects.

  -or-

- Inserting audio effects from a CD.

Keep in mind that audio effects come in a range of file types, some of which are not compatible with PowerPoint 2000. The list below shows the type of audio files that are compatible with PowerPoint 2000.

Compatible PowerPoint 2000 audio file types

AIFF, AIF, AIFC	Audio Interchange File Format
MPEG	Motion Pictures Expert Group
MP3	Layer 3 Motion Pictures
MIDI, MID, RMI	Musical Instrument Digital Interface
WAV	Microsoft Wave
ASF, ASX	Microsoft Streaming Format
CDA	CD Audio

Design Gallery Live contains a variety of items that you can include in your presentation to make it more interesting, including clip art (such as the vegetables used in Chapter 7), photographs, video clips and sound files. In the next exercise, you will use one of the sound files from the gallery. Note that you must have access to the Internet to do this!

Exercise 9.5: Inserting audio effects from *Design Gallery Live*

1) Open EX9.5.PPT.

2) Go to slide 1, 'Green Grocer Group'. Click anywhere in the slide.

3) Choose **Insert | Movies and Sounds | Sound from Gallery**.

4) In the *Insert Sound* dialog box, click the **Clips Online** button.

   Click **OK** to confirm that you have Web access and want to go to the *Design Gallery Live* website.

5) Complete the *Search* area as shown below.

   Click **Go**.

6) Download the *Pizzicato Open* audio clip by clicking the arrow box below its file name.

Clips Online button

The *Pizzicato Open* audio clip is now in the *Microsoft Clip Gallery* on your own computer.

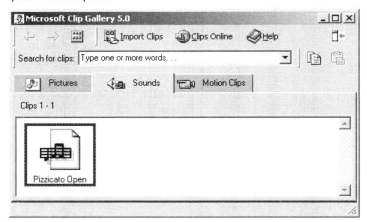

7) Select the audio clip in the *Microsoft Clip Gallery* and choose **Insert clip** from the menu list.

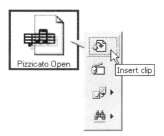

Close the *Insert Sound* dialog box.

PowerPoint asks you if you want the audio clip to play automatically. Click **Yes**.

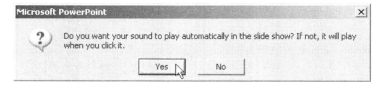

8) Drag the audio icon that appears on slide 1 down to the bottom-right of the screen.

Your audio effect will now play automatically whenever slide 1 is displayed in Slide Show view.

Other audio options

Apart from inserting audio effects from *Design Gallery Live*, you can insert audio effects from other sources, as follows:

■ **Insert an audio effect from local sources**. Most programs, including Office, come with their own selection of audio effects. You usually save these programs to your local disk. To insert such audio effects, choose **Insert | Movies and Sounds | Sound from File**. Then navigate to the file you want to use in the *Insert Sound* dialog box.

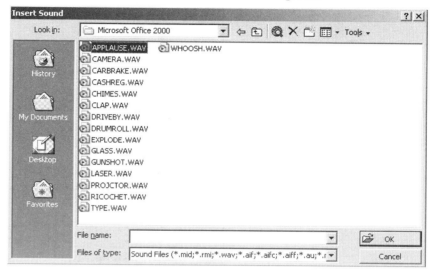

■ **Insert an audio effect from a CD**. To insert a CD audio track, choose **Insert | Movies and Sounds | Play CD Audio Track**. Then follow the instructions in the *Movie and Sound Options* dialog box.

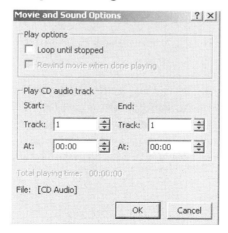

Inserting audio effects from a CD can be a good idea, particularly if you have a song that fits in with the message of your presentation. However, remember that, if the material is copyright, you should first ask permission.

- **Record a voice narration (for all slides)**. To record a voice narration, choose **Slide Show | Record Narration**. Then follow the instructions in the *Record Narration* dialog box.

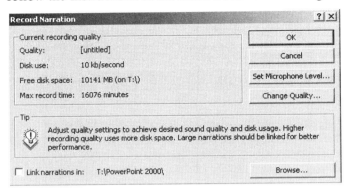

Recording your own audio is especially suitable for Web-based presentations or other self-running slide shows. You will need a computer with a microphone and sound card in order to record.

- **Recording audio effects (for single slides)**. To record an audio effect for a single slide, choose **Insert | Movies and Sounds | Record Sound**. You then follow the instructions in the *Record Sound* dialog box.

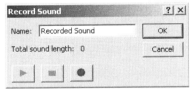

Again, you will need a computer with a microphone and sound card to do this.

Inserting movies

Movies can add to the impact of a presentation. But, as with any animation or illustration, you must ensure that your movie supports your information – a movie that distracts the audience is worse than no movie at all. As with audio files, only certain movie file types are compatible with PowerPoint 2000, as shown opposite.

PowerPoint 2000 compatible movie file types

AVI	Audio Video Interleave
WMV	Windows Media Video
MPEG	Motion Picture Experts Group
QUICKTIME	Apple QuickTime
SWF	Macromedia Shock Wave Flash
ASF/ASX	Microsoft Streaming Format
GIF	Graphic Interchange Format

In the next exercise, we will insert a movie that is in .WMV format.

Exercise 9.6: Inserting movies

1) Open EX9.6.PPT.

2) Go to slide 9, 'What Makes Green Grocer Group'. There's a lot of information on this slide, so you'll need to add a new slide to share it.

   Select bullet points 1 and 2 and press **Ctrl+x** to cut them.

   9 ☐ **What Makes Green Grocer Group?**
   - We believe in environmentally-friendly farming practices
   - We believe our customers deserve the best organic fruit and vegetables

3) Click the **New Slide** button.

4) In the *New Slide* dialog box, select the *Text & Media Clip* slide layout and click **OK**.

   A blank slide 10 now appears.

5) Insert the following text in the title place holder:

   `Company Ethos`

6) Select the text place holder and press **Ctrl+v** to paste the text to the new slide. Your slide should look as shown.

7) Choose **Insert | Movies and Sounds | Movie from File**.

8) In the *Insert Movie* dialog box, navigate to where you have stored the movie file FIELD.WMV.

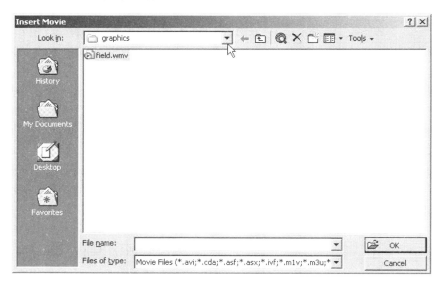

Select the WMV file and click **OK** to insert the movie in the presentation.

9) PowerPoint asks you if you want the movie to play automatically. Click **Yes**.

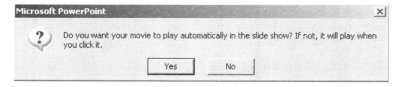

10) View the movie in Slide Show view. (In Normal view, it just appears as a static photograph.) Doesn't it look great!

Note: In the *Custom Animation* dialog box, you can change the order in which the different slide elements appear. You can choose to play the movie before the text or play the movie after the text. The choice is yours!

Animated gif movies

Animated gifs work in the same way as cartoons: a series of graphic images are displayed in rapid succession in order to give the appearance of movement. They are commonly used in presentations and in websites. Animated gifs are sometimes referred to as 'movies'.

In the following exercise you will insert an animated gif from *Design Gallery Live*.

Exercise 9.7: Inserting animated gifs from *Design Gallery Live*

1) Open EX9.7.PPT. Go to the slide number 20, 'Outlook'.

2) Double-click the **Clip Art** icon.

3) In the *Microsoft Clip Gallery* dialog box, click the **Clips Online** button.

Clips Online button

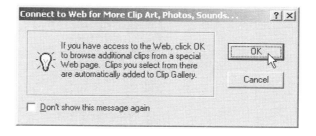

Click **OK** to confirm that you have Web access and want to go to the *Design Gallery Live* website.

4) Complete the *Search* area as shown below.

Click the **Go** button.

5) Download the animated gif shown below by clicking the arrow box underneath its file name.

Select the **Click to Download** button.

The animated gif is now in the *Insert ClipArt* dialog box, contained within your own computer.

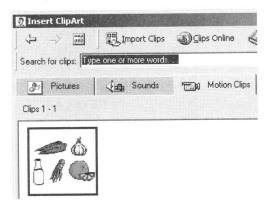

6) Select the animated gif and choose *Insert clip* from the menu list.

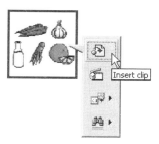

Close the *Insert ClipArt* dialog box. PowerPoint inserts the animated gif in slide number 20.

7) Move the gif to the Clip Art placeholder.

8) Your gif will not be animated in Normal view. Click the **Slide Show** button to see the animation at work.

Your slide should now look as shown.

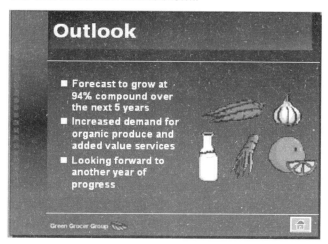

Chapter 9: summary

Animation effects specify how elements in a slide (text, graphics, drawn objects) behave, and the sequence in which they appear.

You can edit the *order* in which the animated elements appear and the *advance method* used, namely *mouse clicking* or *automatic timing*. PowerPoint's *dimming* effect can make your text (or drawn object) change colour, or even disappear from the slide when the next object appears.

You can also animate *charts* in PowerPoint so that series or groups of data points appear in different ways, and in different sequences.

Multimedia effects such as *audio* and *movies* add an extra dimension to your presentation. You can insert audio effects from *local* sources, from *Internet* sources such as the *Design Gallery Live*, from a *CD*, or from your *own recordings*. You can *make* your own movie for the presentation or download one (such as an *animated gif*) from *Design Gallery Live*.

Chapter 9: quick quiz

Circle the correct answer to each of the following questions about animation effects.

Q1	True or false – a WAV file is a movie file.
A.	True.
B.	False.

Q2	To dim bullet points to a specific colour you …
A.	Choose **Slide Show | Custom Animation**. Select the text you want to animate. Under the **Order & Timings** tab, click the sound and motion animations you need. Click the arrow to the right of the *After animation* box and select *More Colors*. Select the colours you need and click **OK**.
B.	Choose **Slide Show | Custom Animation**. Select the text you want to animate. Under the **Multimedia Settings** tab, click the sound and motion animations you need. Click the arrow to the right of the *After animation* box and select *More Colors*. Select the colours you need and click **OK**.
C.	Choose **Slide Show | Custom Animation**. Select the text you want to animate. Under the **Effects** tab, click the sound and motion animations you need. Click the arrow to the right of the *After animation* box and select *More Colors*. Select the colours you need and click **OK**.
D.	Choose **Slide Show | Custom Animation**. Select the text you want to animate. Under the **Chart Effects** tab, click the sound and motion animations you need. Click the arrow to the right of the *After animation* box and select *More Colors*. Select the colours you need and click **OK**.

Q3	To insert an audio effect from *Design Gallery Live* you ...
A.	Choose **Insert | Movies and Sound | Sound from File**. Click the **Clips Online** button in the Insert Sound dialog box. Click **OK** to access the *Design Gallery Live* website.
B.	Choose **Insert | Movies and Sound | Sound from Gallery**. Click the **Import Clips** button in the *Insert Sound* dialog box. Click **OK** to access the *Design Gallery Live* website.
C.	Choose **Insert | Movies and Sound | Record Sound**. Click the **Clips Online** button in the *Insert Sound* dialog box. Click **OK** to access the *Design Gallery Live* website.
D.	Choose **Insert | Movies and Sound | Sound from Gallery**. Click the **Clips Online** button in the *Insert Sound* dialog box. Click **OK** to access the *Design Gallery Live* website.

Q4	To insert a movie from your local disk, you ...
A.	Choose **Insert | Movies and Sound | Clipart**.
B.	Choose **Insert | Movies and Sound | Movie from Gallery**.
C.	Choose **Insert | Movies and Sound | Record Movie**.
D.	Choose **Insert | Movies and Sound | Movie from File**.

Answers

1: B, **2:** C, **3:** D, **4:** D.

10

Graphic editing and graphic effects

A picture is worth a thousand words – and you will communicate your message much more effectively if you support your text with relevant graphics. You have already seen how to insert Clip Art images and charts into your presentation. In this chapter, we will look in more detail at graphic editing and graphic effects. Typically, editing a graphic involves changing its position or orientation on the slide, cropping it so that only a part of the original is seen, and making it bigger or smaller. Other effects are available: you can place a shadow behind an image; you can turn flat objects into 3-D; you can make an image semi-transparent, so that text can be read 'through' it. And, depending on the graphics software you have available to you, you can alter the image by blurring or sharpening it, bending or stretching it, and applying a wide range of special effects. You can also convert the image from colour to shades of grey or black-and-white, and change its colour depth and file format.

New skills

At the end of this chapter you should be able to:

- Edit a graphic
- Crop a graphic
- Flip, mirror and rotate a graphic
- Apply different effects to a graphic
- Convert graphics to different file formats

New words

At the end of this chapter you should be able to explain the following terms:

- Cropping
- Greyscaling

Syllabus reference

This chapter covers the following syllabus points:

- AM 6.3.1.1
- AM 6.3.2.1
- AM 6.3.2.2
- AM 6.3.2.3
- AM 6.3.2.5
- AM 6.3.3.1
- AM 6.3.3.2
- AM 6.3.3.3
- AM 6.3.3.4
- AM 6.3.3.5
- AM 6.3.3.6

Moving graphics

In Chapter 4, you repositioned graphics in two ways: by dragging the graphic with the mouse, and by using the *Format AutoShape* command to specify a precise position for the graphic, using co-ordinates.

Both methods can be applied to any PowerPoint object – placeholders, drawn objects, AutoShapes or pictures – on your slide. The most common method is the simpler one of dragging. You might want to use co-ordinates if you need to align objects precisely in a certain way, or if you wanted to use exactly the same placement of objects on different slides. To use the co-ordinate method, right-click on the object, choose **Format AutoShape** (or **Format Picture**, or **Format Placeholder**, or whatever), and click on the **Position** tab. You can then specify the distance that the object should be located from the edge or the centre of the slide.

Cropping graphics

If you want to eliminate parts of an imported picture from your slide, in order to focus your audience's attention on a specific part of it, you *crop* it. PowerPoint's cropping tool is on the *Picture* toolbar. If the *Picture* toolbar is not displayed, either choose **View | Toolbars | Picture**, or right-click on the picture and choose **Show Picture Toolbar** from the pop-up menu. (Note that you cannot crop AutoShapes or placeholders.)

Crop button

Exercise 10.1: Cropping a picture

1) Open EX10.1.PPT, and go to slide number 14, 'Organic Farming Practices'.

2) Select the graphic and then click the **Crop** button in the *Picture* toolbar. (If the *Picture* toolbar is not displayed, choose **View | Toolbars | Picture**.)

3) Move the mouse pointer over any of the eight sizing handles on the picture. Notice how the pointer changes shape.

4) Drag the handle into the picture. As you drag, the cropped area is represented by a dotted line.

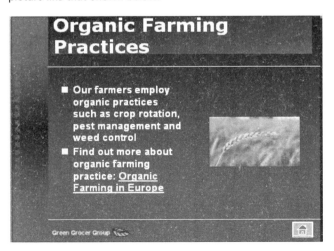

Release the mouse button when the part of the picture you want to eliminate is outside the dotted line.

5) Repeat this for each edge of the picture until you are left with a picture like that shown below.

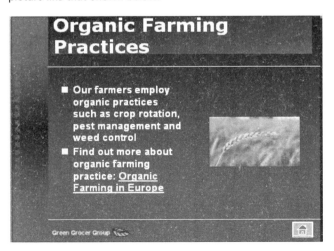

Resizing graphics

You can resize any graphic object (drawn object, AutoShape, imported Clip Art or picture) as described in Chapter 3, by clicking on it and dragging one of its sizing handles. Using the corner handles resizes the object proportionately (the object grows or shrinks without distorting). Using the handles in the middle of the sides grows or shrinks the object in one dimension only – the object is stretched or squashed.

Exercise 10.2: Enlarging a picture

1) Open EX10.2.PPT, and go to slide number 14, 'Organic Farming Practices'.

2) Select the picture that you cropped in Exercise 10.1.

Notice how the sizing handles appear.

3) Drag one of the corner sizing handles to enlarge the picture so that it fills the space on the right of the slide, as shown below.

Well done! You've now successfully enlarged a graphic!

Flipping and rotating

The *Flip* and *Rotate* effects change the orientation of a graphic object on your slide.

- *Flip* (also known as *Mirror* in some graphics programs) creates a mirror image of the graphic. If you flip horizontally, you create a horizontal mirror image (in which the vertical axis remains constant): what was left is now right. If you flip vertically, you create a vertical mirror image: what was up is now down. Note that if you repeat the operation, you are back where you started.

- *Rotate* turns the graphic clockwise or anti-clockwise. PowerPoint offers you the option of rotating the graphic 90° either way, or of applying *Free Rotate*, in which you can rotate the object as much or as little as you like. Note that if you repeat the 90° rotation four times, you are back where you started.

Try flipping and rotating in the following exercise.

Exercise 10.3: Flipping and rotating a graphic

1) Open EX10.3.PPT, and go to slide number 11, 'Traceability', and select the arrow AutoShape.

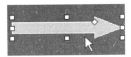

2) If the *Drawing* toolbar is not displayed at the bottom of the screen, choose **View | Toolbars | Drawing**. On the *Drawing* toolbar, choose **Draw | Rotate or Flip | Rotate Left**. Notice that the arrow now points upwards.

3) Repeat step 2. Notice that the arrow now points to the left.

4) With the arrow still selected, choose **Draw | Rotate or Flip | Flip Horizontal**. Notice that the arrow has turned around, and now points to the right again.

Because the shapes in the slide are symmetrical, the different effects of flipping and rotating may not be apparent. They will become more obvious in the next exercise.

Exercise 10.4: Free rotating a graphic

1) In EX10.4.PPT, go to slide number 11, 'Traceability'.

2) Click the arrow AutoShape. Choose **Draw | Rotate or Flip | Free Rotate**, or click the **Free Rotate** button on the *Drawing* toolbar. Notice that the sizing handles on the arrow AutoShape have changed into green circles – rotating handles.

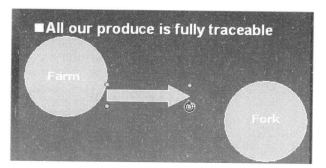

3) Click one of the rotating handles and drag it. Notice that, while you are dragging, the new position of the arrow is indicated by dotted lines.

Position the arrow as shown below.

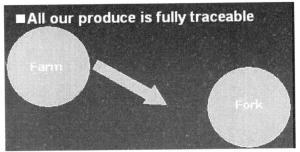

4) Now repeat the rotating and flipping exercises: choose
Draw | Rotate or Flip | Rotate Left. Notice that the arrow now
points up to the right, at 90° to the original.

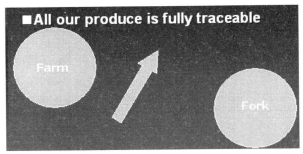

5) Repeat step 4. Rotating twice in the same direction turns the object
through 180°, so that the arrow now points up and to the left (the
opposite of its starting direction).

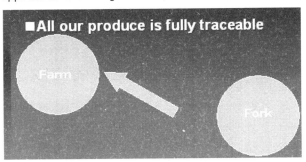

6) With the arrow still selected, choose **Draw | Rotate or Flip | Flip
Horizontal**. Notice that the arrow has turned around, and now points
to the right, but upwards, not downwards – it has been flipped around
the vertical axis.

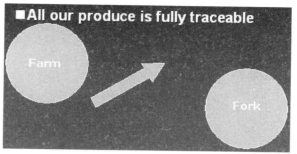

7) Change the arrow back to its starting position. Choose **Draw | Rotate or Flip | Flip Vertical**.

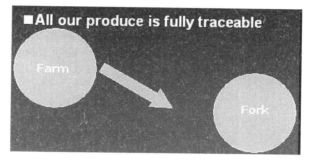

Converting pictures to drawn objects

Only certain kinds of graphic can be flipped and rotated: objects drawn in PowerPoint, using the drawing tools or AutoShapes, and imported objects that can be converted into a PowerPoint object or group.

If, when you select an object to rotate or flip, you find that all the options on the **Draw | Rotate or Flip** menu are greyed out, try to convert the object to a PowerPoint group, as in Exercise 9.5 below. Only certain kinds of graphic can be converted in this way – much Clip Art can be converted, but photos and other bitmaps, for example, cannot. If your graphic can't be converted, and you really want to flip or rotate it, your only option is to open the graphic in another graphics package, edit it there and then re-import it into your presentation.

Exercise 10.5: Converting a picture to a drawn object

1) Open EX10.5.PPT, and go to slide number 12, 'Our Fruit and Vegetables', and click the imported Clip Art image of the cabbage.

2) Choose **Draw | Rotate or Flip**, and notice that there are no options available to you.

3) Now choose **Draw | Ungroup**, and click **Yes** to confirm that you want to convert the picture to a Microsoft Office object. Notice that each tiny segment of the cabbage is converted into a separate object that can be manipulated in PowerPoint: you can move it around, enlarge or shrink it, stretch it – or rotate or flip it. For the moment, however, leave the entire group of objects selected.

4) Choose **Draw | Group**.

You can now treat the graphic as a PowerPoint object – all the options on the **Draw | Rotate or Flip** menu are available. Experiment with the cabbage, by rotating and flipping it.

Applying PowerPoint effects

You already know how to apply many PowerPoint effects. However, there are other effects that you can experiment with, such as:

- **Shadow**. This creates a background shadow behind the object, text or graphic.

- **3-D**. This adds a third dimension to a drawn object.

- **Semi-transparent**. This makes the drawn object or graphic semi-transparent, so that, for example, underlying text can be read through it.

Exercise 10.6: Create a shadow behind an object

1) Open EX10.6.PPT, and go to slide number 12, 'Our Fruit and Vegetables', and click the image of the apples.

Shadow button

2) Click the **Shadow** button on the *Drawing* toolbar.

3) Select the *Shadow Style 2* option from the **Shadow** menu.

The apples should now look as shown.

4) Click the **Shadow** button again, and select the *Shadow Settings* option.

The *Shadow Settings* toolbar now appears.

5) Use the buttons on the *Shadow Settings* toolbar to adjust the shadow effect – you can reveal more or less of the shadow by moving it up, down, left or right, and you can change its colour. Experiment with these options.

If you want to remove a shadow from an object, choose the *No Shadow* option on the **Shadow** menu, or click the **Shadow On/Off** button on the *Shadow Settings* toolbar.

Exercise 10.7: Make an object 3-D

1) Open EX10.7.PPT, and go to slide number 11, 'Traceability', and select the arrow between the two circles.

3-D Button

2) Click the **3-D** button on the *Drawing* toolbar.

3) Select the *3-D Style 1* option from the **3-D** menu.

The arrow should now look as shown.

4) Click the **3-D** button and select the *3-D Settings* option.

The *3-D Settings* toolbar now appears.

5) Use the buttons on the *3-D Settings* toolbar to adjust the 3-D effect, by tilting the arrow down, up, left or right, changing its depth and direction, and changing the angle of lighting, the surface texture and the colour. Experiment with these options.

To make it look like the one shown below:

- Leave the *Tilt* settings unchanged.

- Under *Depth*, choose 36 point.

- Under *Direction*, choose *Perspective*.

- Under *Lighting*, choose the top right.

- Under *Surface*, choose *Metal*.

- Under *3-D Color*, choose a light blue.

To remove a 3-D effect from an object, choose the *No 3-D* option on the **3-D** menu, or click the **3-D On/Off** button on the *3-D Settings* toolbar.

Note: You can apply the 3-D effect only to PowerPoint objects and imported objects that have been converted to PowerPoint objects.

Once you have manipulated the effects to your liking on one object, you can use the Format Painter to apply the same effects to other objects – as shown in the next exercise.

Exercise 10.8: Copy the style of one object and apply it to another

1) Open EX10.8.PPT, and go to slide number 11, 'Traceability', and click the arrow between the two circles.

2) With the arrow selected, click the **Format Painter** button on the *Formatting* toolbar. Notice that your cursor turns into a paint brush.

3) Click on the left-hand circle. Notice that it becomes a 3-D object with the same characteristics as the arrow.

4) Repeat steps 2 and 3 with the right-hand circle.

Your slide should now look as shown.

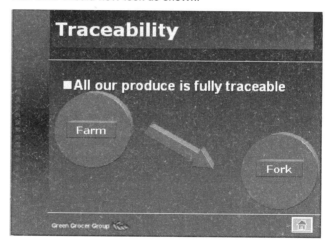

Exercise 10.9: Making an object semi-transparent

1) Open EX10.8.PPT, and go to slide number 11, 'Traceability'.

2) Right-click on the right-hand circle; choose **Grouping | Ungroup** from the pop-up menu; click anywhere outside the circle.

3) Right-click on the 'Fork' box; choose **Order | Send to Back** from the pop-up menu; click anywhere outside the circle.

4) Right-click on the circle; choose **Format | AutoShape** from the pop-up menu. The *Format AutoShape* dialog box is displayed.

5) On the *Colors and Lines* tab, select the *Semitransparent* check box and click **OK**.

Notice the effect on the drawing.

6) Open EX10.9.PPT, and go to slide number 12, 'Our Fruit and Vegetables'; right-click the image of the cabbage. (Remember that you converted this image to a PowerPoint object in Exercise 9.5 – you can apply the semi-transparent effect only to objects created in PowerPoint or ones that have been converted.)

7) From the pop-up menu, choose *Format Object*.

The *Format Object* dialog box is displayed. As above, select the *Semitransparent* check box on the *Colors and Lines* tab, and click **OK**.

Notice the effect on the image of the cabbage.

8) Click the image of the cabbage and drag it over the text on the left of the slide. Notice that you can now read the text through the cabbage!

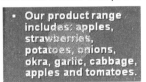

If the object you want to make semi-transparent is an unconverted Clip Art picture or a scanned photograph, click the **Image Control** button on the *Picture* toolbar and click *Watermark*.

Exercise 10.10: Making parts of an object transparent

1) Open EX10.10.PPT, and go to slide number 1, the title slide, and right-click the logo. If the *Picture* toolbar is not displayed, choose **View | Toolbars | Picture**.

2) Click the **Set Transparent Color** button in the *Picture* toolbar. Notice that the mouse pointer changes shape.

Set Transparent Color button

3) Click the white area between the circular logo and the edges of the square. The white is eliminated, and the background colour or pattern shows through.

This feature is particularly useful for integrating graphics into your slides.

Note: The transparent effect is available only for certain kinds of graphics. Only one colour in a picture can be made transparent – this means that in a scanned photograph, for example, the transparent effect may not be noticeable, as what appears to be a single colour may in fact be composed of a range of colours, each slightly different from the next.

Adjusting the colour of images

There are three main reasons why you might want to alter the colours in your images:

- To enhance the picture and make the details in it easier to see.

- To make the picture harmonize with the colours in your presentation, or with other pictures.

- To reduce the file size of the picture, so that it takes up less disk space, loads more quickly, or can be e-mailed more easily.

Of course, you can also adjust the colours simply because it's fun, and can result in more interesting images. In the exercises below, you will adjust the contrast and brightness of an image, make colour substitutions in an image, and change the colour depth of an image.

Exercise 10.11: Adjusting brightness and contrast

1) Open EX10.11.PPT, and go to slide number 14, 'Our Farmers'.

2) Select the graphic and click several times on the **More Contrast** button in the *Picture* toolbar.

Notice how the picture changes as you click.

3) With the picture still selected, click several times on the **Less Brightness** button. You can continue to adjust the contrast and brightness of the picture, using the **More Contrast**, **Less Contrast**, **More Brightness** and **Less Brightness** buttons, until you are happy with the result.

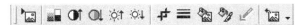

**Reset Picture
button**

4) Click the **Reset Picture** button to get back to the original picture.
(If you reset the picture, it will be restored to its original size – you
will have to enlarge it again.)

In the previous exercise you worked on contrast and brightness;
in the next exercise you will work on black-and-white shades.

Exercise 10.12: Converting a colour image to black-and-white

1) Open EX10.12.PPT, and go to slide number 12, 'Our Fruit and Vegetables'.

2) Select the potatoes graphic and click the **Image Control** button on
the *Picture* toolbar.

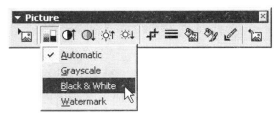

3) Select the *Black & White* option.

The picture of the potatoes is now changed to black-and-white.

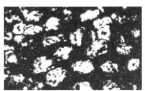

Clearly, this is not something you would do very often – black-
and-white images (without any grey) are very stark, and it is
difficult to interpret the picture. However, it is sometimes useful
to convert a scanned document to black-and-white, as it
maximizes the contrast, and can make the document more
legible. Another way to make a graphic more legible is to
convert it to greyscale.

Greyscaling and colour resolution

Graphics are made up of dots called pixels, or picture elements. Each pixel is represented in the computer by a number of bits. The greater the number of colours in the picture, the more bits are needed to represent each pixel. This means that graphics that use a wide colour palette are bigger files, and bigger files means that the files take longer to load, display and transmit.

There is a trade-off between colour depth and file size. One solution is to greyscale your graphics. When you greyscale a graphic, you convert all its pixels to shades of grey.

Whereas a full colour picture typically draws on a palette of 16 million colours (24-bit pixels), a greyscaled graphic typically contains pixels made up of 256 shades of grey, and each pixel is represented by eight bits.

Exercise 10.13: Converting a graphic to greyscale

1) Open EX10.13.PPT, and go to slide number 12, 'Our Fruit and Vegetables'.

2) Select the picture of the potatoes.

3) Click the **Image Control** button on the *Picture* toolbar, and select the *Grayscale* option.

The picture of the potatoes is now changed to shades of grey.

This is a much better option – the potatoes are easy to see. You might use this option if you want to include a number of photos in your presentation, some of which are colour and some black-and-white (in the normal sense). Applying the greyscale effect to the colour photos will make them all consistent in style.

More sophisticated graphic effects

If you want to change a graphic more radically, PowerPoint may not be the tool for you. There is a very wide range of programs available with graphic editing capabilities.

Microsoft Paint

Microsoft Paint (which comes with Windows 2000) is a fairly simple program that enables you to skew an image, which is an interesting effect. To do this, open the graphic in Paint, and choose **Image | Stretch/Skew**. Experiment with *low* numbers for horizontal and vertical skew (try 5).

More usefully, Paint allows you to reduce the colour depth of an image by choosing **File | Save As**, and selecting from the *Save as Type* drop-down list. You can reduce the file size significantly, but you may lose detail in the picture. For example, the file size of a typical picture would vary as follows, depending on the format in which it was saved:

Format	File size
24-bit Bitmap (16 million colours)	119 KB
256 colour Bitmap (8-bit colour)	41 KB
Graphics Interchange Format (gif)	28 KB
16 colour Bitmap (4-bit colour)	21 KB
JPEG File Interchange Format (jpg)	10 KB
Monochrome Bitmap	6 KB

Adobe Photoshop

Adobe Photoshop is the favoured tool among graphic designers for editing and adding effects to graphics. (You can download a trial version of this graphics editing application from www.adobe.com.) It has many effects that you can apply to graphics – you can blur or sharpen the image, apply line-drawing or painting effects, shape your graphic with effects like *Twirl* and *Spherize*, or alter it further with effects like *Stained Glass* and *Embossing*. It's worth taking the time to explore the program to see its capabilities. For example, try the next exercise.

Exercise 10.14: Experimenting with Adobe Photoshop

1) Open Adobe Photoshop. Choose **File | Open** and navigate to BOWL1.JPG. Select the graphic and click **Open**.

2) Choose **Filter | Sketch | Charcoal**.

3) Click **OK** in the *Charcoal* dialog box.

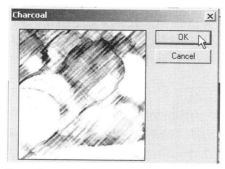

Your photograph now becomes a charcoal drawing. If this seems a little dark for your presentation, add the *Chalk & Charcoal* effect to lighten it up.

4) Choose **Filter | Sketch | Chalk & Charcoal**.

5) Click **OK** in the *Chalk & Charcoal* dialog box.

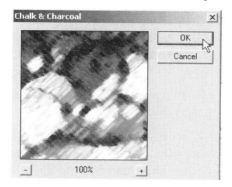

Your photograph now becomes a chalk and charcoal drawing.

6) Save the graphic as BOWL2.JPG.

7) Open EX10.14.PPT and insert the chalk and charcoal drawing into slide 5, 'Our Mission Statement'.

Your slide should now look as shown.

Chapter 10: summary

You can edit the size of a graphic by *cropping* it. You can use a Graphics Editor to do this but you can also use the *Picture* toolbar in PowerPoint to crop and *resize* a graphic.

Change the positioning of your graphic by *flipping*, *mirroring* and *rotating* it. As well as changing the physical size of a graphic, you can also *convert it to an object*. This is useful when you want to change a Clip Art picture into a drawn object.

PowerPoint comes with a range of graphic effects. For example, if you want to add more depth to a graphic you can apply a *shadow effect*. You can apply different shadow types and different shadow colours. Go even further by applying *3-D effects* to a graphic. Another useful effect is to make a graphic *semi-transparent* or parts of it transparent. (This is mostly used when integrating graphics into a slide.)

Tweak the look of your graphics by adjusting the colours. You can apply graphic *effects* such as *greyscaling*, *converting to black and white* and *changing contrast*.

If you want to change the size of a graphic file, you save it in a different *file format*. For example, you can open a .BMP image and save it as a .JPG.

Lastly, you can use other graphic editors like Adobe Photoshop or Microsoft Paint. A good experiment is to make a photograph look like a line drawing by applying Adobe Photoshop's *Chalk & Charcoal* effect.

Chapter 10: quick quiz

Circle the correct answer to each of the following questions about graphic editing and effects.

Q1	To make a right-facing arrow turn to the left you choose ...
A.	Draw | Rotate or Flip | **Flip Vertical**.
B.	Draw | Rotate or Flip | **Rotate Left**.
C.	Draw | Rotate or Flip | **Rotate Right**.
D.	Draw | Rotate or Flip | **Flip Horizontal**.

Q2	To convert a Clip Art graphic to a drawn object, you choose …
A.	**Draw	Change AutoShape** and click **Yes** to confirm conversion.
B.	**Draw	Order	Bring to Front** and click **Yes** to confirm conversion.
C.	**Draw	Ungroup** and click **Yes** to confirm conversion.
D.	**Draw	Group** and click **Yes** to confirm conversion.

Q3	In PowerPoint, what *Picture* toolbar button is used to crop a graphic?
A.	
B.	
C.	
D.	

Q4	In PowerPoint, what *Picture* toolbar button is used to make parts of an object transparent?
A.	
B.	
C.	
D.	

Answers

1: D, **2:** C, **3:** B, **4:** A.

11 Linking

In this chapter

Often, when you are creating a PowerPoint presentation, you want to use information that you have generated in another application – a Word document, an Excel worksheet or chart, or an Access database, for example. The most obvious way of doing this is to simply copy the information from the other application and paste it into your PowerPoint slide. In this chapter, you will learn about other ways of getting information from external sources into your PowerPoint presentation – by linking and by embedding.

New skills

At the end of this chapter you should be able to:

- Embed information from an external application into a presentation

- Link information from an external application into a presentation

- Display linked or embedded information as an icon

- Display linked or embedded information as an object

- Edit linked information

- Edit embedded information

New words

At the end of this chapter you should be able to explain the following terms:

- Embedded objects

- Linked objects

- Source files

This chapter covers the following syllabus points:

- AM 6.7.1.1

- AM 6.7.1.2

- AM 6.7.1.3

- AM 6.7.1.4

Multiple sources of information

When you are preparing your presentation, you might include information from a variety of sources, such as:

- An Excel spreadsheet.

- An Access database.

- A Word document.

- A graphic.

- Another PowerPoint presentation.

There might, for example, be relevant information about the Green Grocer Group in a financial spreadsheet.

Two situations arise:

- You want the presentation to reflect the financial position on the date you created it. In other words, you don't want to update the presentation when the spreadsheet subsequently changes.

  -or-

- You want the presentation to change when the numbers change in the spreadsheet, so that it always automatically reflects the latest financial situation.

With PowerPoint, you handle each of these situations differently.

Copying and pasting

If you simply copy the information from the spreadsheet and paste it into PowerPoint, the two copies are entirely independent – you can change one without affecting the other. However, the only tools you have at your disposal for changing the information that you have pasted into your presentation are PowerPoint tools – these might be fine for straightforward text, but if the information is in the form of a table, a worksheet or a chart, they are a bit limited.

Embedding

If you want to make the information in your presentation independent from the information in your worksheet, but you want to update it using the tools with which it was created, you need to embed the information in the presentation.

Linking

If you want to keep the information in the two applications synchronized, you need to link them. With linking, there is actually only one copy of the information. What appears in your PowerPoint presentation is a temporary graphic representation of the information. Changes can be made to the information only in the original application, and these changes are immediately reflected in the PowerPoint representation.

Embedded information

Information embedded in a PowerPoint slide is a copy of the original information. However, unlike copies made with the usual copy and paste functions, embedded information 'remembers' the application in which it was created. When you edit the embedded information, you are presented with the menus and toolbars of the original application. For example, when you edit an Excel worksheet embedded in a PowerPoint presentation, the PowerPoint menu bar and toolbars are temporarily replaced by the Excel menu bar and toolbars. However, the two copies are independent – if you change the copy that you have embedded in a slide, the original is unaffected, and if you change the original, the one embedded in your slide is unaffected.

You can present your embedded information either in full (as an object), or as an icon. You might choose to present it as an icon, for example, if your audience is going to view the presentation online and the embedded object is a large spreadsheet that would have to be very much reduced in size to fit on a slide.

In the exercise below, you will embed an Access database in your presentation, and show it as an icon. The same procedure can be used to embed a chart, a worksheet, a document, or a graphic in a slide.

Exercise 11.1: Embedding information

1) Open EX11.1.PPT.

2) Select slide 18, 'Best Sellers'.

3) Choose **Insert | Object**.

4) In the *Insert Object* dialog box, select the *Create from file* option.

5) Click the **Browse** button, and navigate to the Access database GREEN GROCER GROUP.MDB. Click **OK**.

6) Select the *Display as icon* check box.

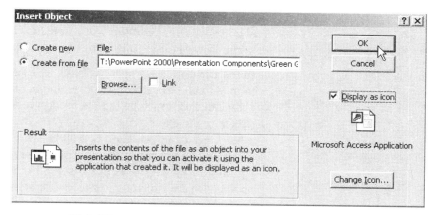

Click **OK**.

The **Access** icon now appears in the centre of the slide.

7) Move the icon to the bottom-left of the slide (use the arrow keys or drag-and-drop). If you wish, you can change the size of the icon by clicking on it and dragging one of its sizing handles.

Your screen should now look as shown.

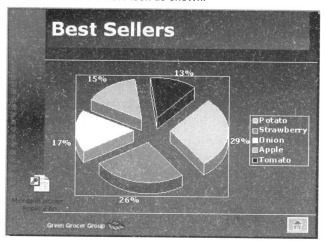

Linked information

Linked information in a PowerPoint slide is represented in the slide by a graphic object. The graphic may be an icon, or it may be a full-sized representation of the original document. In either case, the graphic provides a link to the original document in the original application. For example, in PowerPoint, to edit a linked Excel worksheet, you click on the graphic representation of it and the worksheet opens in Excel. Any changes you make to the worksheet are reflected immediately in the PowerPoint representation.

In the exercise below, you will link an Excel worksheet to a slide in the Green Grocer Group presentation, and show it as an icon. (You can choose which icon is used to represent the worksheet, as shown in the exercise.) The same procedure can be used to link other kinds of information to a slide, such as a Word document, a database, another PowerPoint presentation, or a graphic. To link to a graphic you simply choose **Insert | Picture | From File**. You navigate to the file you require and select it. Click the arrow to the right of the **Insert** button and select *Link to File*.

Exercise 11.2: Linking a worksheet to a slide

1) Open EX11.2.PPT.

2) Select slide 17, 'End of Year Results'.

3) Choose **Insert | Object**.

4) In the *Insert Object* dialog box, select the *Create from file* option.

5) Click the **Browse** button and navigate to the Excel worksheet SUPPLIERS.XLS. Click **OK**.

6) In the *Insert Object* dialog box, select the *Link* check box.

7) Select the *Display as icon* check box.

8) Click the **Change Icon** button.

Change Icon button

Select the alternative Excel worksheet icon (as below) from the range shown and click **OK**.

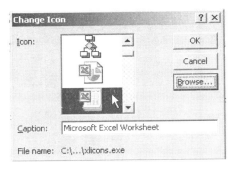

9) Click **OK** in the *Insert Object* dialog box.

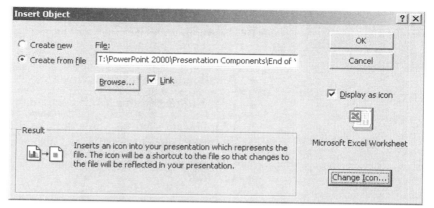

The Excel worksheet icon now appears in the centre of the slide.

10) Move the icon to the bottom-left of the slide. If you wish, you can change the size of the icon by clicking on it and dragging one of its sizing handles.

Your screen should now look as shown.

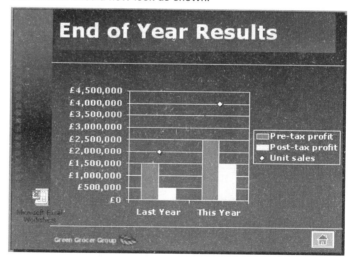

Linking part of a source file

In the previous two exercises, you represented the embedded and linked files as icons in your slides. That made sense: if the worksheet or the database table were shown in full as objects in the slides, they would have been too small to read. Most of the time, however, and particularly if you are projecting your slides, you will select a small part of the source document and show it as an object on the slide, instead of trying to show your audience the entire document.

You can embed or link a part of almost any document –
for example:

- An Excel chart.

- A cell range from an Excel worksheet.

- A line of text from a Word document.

In the following exercise, you will link selected text in a Word
document to your presentation and display it as an object. You
will use the same procedure to link a selected range of cells in
a worksheet.

Exercise 11.3: Linking part of a source file

1) Open EX11.3.PPT.

2) Select slide 17, 'End of Year Results'.

3) Click the **New Slide** button, and select the *Title Only* slide layout in
the *New Slide* dialog box. Click **OK**.

4) Type the following in the title placeholder of the new slide 17:

What Our Customers Say

5) Open Word, and open WHAT OUR CUSTOMERS SAY.DOC.

6) Select the first two paragraphs below the heading (see below), and
press **Ctrl+c** to copy them.

"I've never had such a range of organic fruit
and vegetables available to me before."

"What I really like about Greeen Grocer Group
is their dependability. When they say they
deliver, they actually deliver, on time and to
order."

"Our customers are still talking about the taste

7) In PowerPoint, in slide 17, choose **Edit | Paste Special**. The *Paste
Special* dialog box appears.

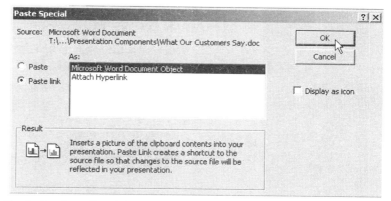

8) In the *Paste Special* dialog box, select *Paste link*. Ensure that Microsoft Word Document Object is selected in the *As* box. If necessary, deselect the *Display as icon* check box – you want to display the text in full, as an object, not as an icon. Click **OK**.

Your slide should now look as shown.

9) Click the **New Slide** button, select the *Title Only* slide layout, and click **OK**.

10) Give the new slide a title: Top Three Producers

11) Open Excel, and open the file SUPPLIERS.XLS.

12) Select the nine cells B2 to D4, and press **Ctrl + c** to copy them to the Clipboard.

13) In PowerPoint, choose **Edit | Paste Special**, and in the Paste Special dialog box, select *Paste Link*. This time, make sure that Microsoft Excel Worksheet Object is selected. Click **OK**.

Note that The text is displayed in PowerPoint exactly as it was created in Word or Excel. In the first slide you created, it is a reasonable point size (26 point), but the black font does not work well against the dark background. In the next exercise, you will edit some of the text, and change the font colour.

Exercise 11.4: Editing a linked file

1) Open EX11.4.PPT. Go to slide 18, 'What Our Customers Say'.

2) Double-click the linked text, or right-click it and choose **Linked Document Object | Edit**.

   The original document opens in Microsoft Word.

3) Change the spelling mistake:

   'Greeen' becomes 'Green'

   about Greeen Grocer Group

4) Select the first two paragraphs, as before, and choose **Format | Font**.

5) In the *Font* dialog box, click the arrow to the right of the *Font color* box and select the white colour. Click **OK**.

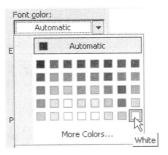

6) In PowerPoint, notice that the text in slide 18 has changed.

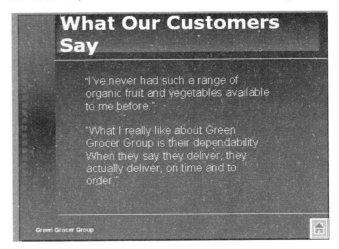

Congratulations! You've linked selected text from a Word document to your presentation, and seen how, when you change the text in Word, the changes are automatically reflected in PowerPoint.

Editing links

Not only can you change the linked information, you can also change the links themselves, in two ways:

- You can change the source file used for the information, as in Exercise 11.5.

- You can break the link, so that the information in your presentation is embedded, rather than linked, as in Exercise 11.6.

Exercise 11.5: Linking to a different source file

1) Open EX11.5.PPT.

2) Choose **Edit | Links**.

3) In the *Links* dialog box, select the Worksheet link.

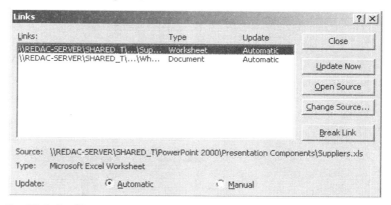

4) Click the **Change Source** button. Navigate to END OF YEAR RESULTS.XLS and click **Open**.

5) In the *Links* dialog box, click the **Close** button.

6) Check the effect of this change: go to slide 17, 'End of Year Results'; double-click the Excel icon, and note that the END OF YEAR RESULTS.XLS spreadsheet opens in Excel.

Converting linked objects into embedded objects

If you no longer want your presentation to be updated automatically when the source document changes, you need to break the link. Remember, however, that the linked document is represented in your slide either by an icon, or by a graphic representation of the source document. When you break the link between the representation on your slide and the source document, you are left with a graphic – either an icon or a 'picture' of the source document. This graphic representation can be edited only within PowerPoint – it does not 'remember' the application in which it was originally created.

Exercise 11.6: Converting a linked object to an embedded object

1) Open EX11.6.PPT.

2) Choose **Edit | Links**.

3) In the *Links* dialog box, select the Document link.

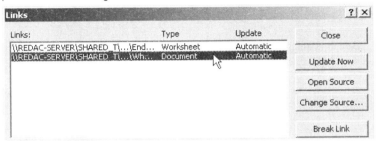

4) Click the **Break Link** button, then click the **Close** button.

5) Go to slide 18, 'What Our Customers Say'. Double-click on the text.

6) PowerPoint asks if you want to convert the linked object. Click the **Yes** button.

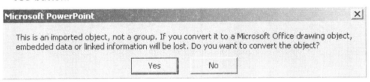

Note: The text is presented in a number of text boxes, each of which can be edited separately – for example, you can modify the text, or change the font size.

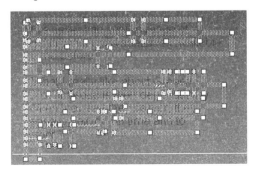

7) In the *Drawing* toolbar, click the arrow to the right of the **Font Color** button, and choose a yellow colour. The text in the slide changes colour (but the text in the original document is unchanged).

"I've never had such a range of organic fruit and vegetables available to me before."

"What I really like about Green Grocer Group is their dependability. When they say they deliver, they actually deliver, on time and to order."

Note: If you break the link from an icon to a source document, the icon still appears as a graphic object in the presentation – the data to which it referred does not appear.

Converting between an icon and an object

If you first chose to represent the source document as an icon, and subsequently wish to represent it in full as an object, right-click the icon, choose **Linked Worksheet Object | Convert** (or similar, depending on the source document type). In the *Convert* dialog box, deselect the *Display as icon* check box.

Similarly, if you first chose to represent the source document in full as an object, and subsequently wish to represent it as an icon, right-click the document representation in the slide, choose **Linked Worksheet Object | Convert**. In the *Convert* dialog box, select the *Display as icon* check box.

Where to keep your linked documents

PowerPoint needs to find a linked document in order to display it. For this reason, it's best to keep your linked documents in the same folder as your presentation. If you are copying your presentation to CD or to a floppy disk, make sure to copy any linked documents at the same time.

Chapter 11: summary

You can include information from many sources in a PowerPoint presentation. If you *embed* such information, the copy in your PowerPoint slide is independent of the original, but you can use the features of the original application to edit the information. If you *link* the information, PowerPoint shows a graphic representation of the original information, but all editing is done to the source document in the original application, and the graphic representation in PowerPoint is updated with any changes.

In either case, you can choose to show the information in full as an *object* or as an *icon* – double-clicking the icon opens the full embedded or linked document.

You can embed and link both *files* and selected *parts of files*, such as pieces of text, cells in a worksheet, or charts.

You can *change* the source file for a link, and you can *convert* a linked object to an embedded object.

Chapter 11: quick quiz

Circle the correct answer to each of the following multiple-choice questions about linking and embedding objects and icons.

Q1	To embed an information type as an icon you ...
A.	Choose **Insert | Object**, browse to your selected file, and click **OK**. Select the *Link* check box and select the *Display as icon* check box. Click **OK**.
B.	Choose **Insert | Object**, browse to your selected file, and click **OK**. Deselect the *Link* check box and select the *Display as icon* check box. Click **OK**.
C.	Choose **Insert | Object**, browse to your selected file, and click **OK**. Deselect the *Link* check box and deselect the *Display as icon* check box. Click **OK**.
D.	Choose **Insert | Object**, browse to your selected file. Deselect the *Link* check box and select the *Display as icon* check box. Click **OK**.

Q2	To insert part of a document as an icon you ...
A.	Copy the information that you need from the source file. Return to your PowerPoint presentation slide and choose **Insert | Paste Special**. In the *Paste Special* dialog box you select *Paste link* and Microsoft Word Document Object. Select the *Display as icon* check box and click **OK**.
B.	Copy the information that you need from the source file. Return to your PowerPoint presentation slide and choose **Edit | Paste Special**. In the *Paste Special* dialog box you select *Paste* and Microsoft Word Document Object. Select the *Display as icon* check box and click **OK**.
C.	Copy the information that you need from the source file. Return to your PowerPoint presentation slide and choose **Edit | Paste Special**. In the *Paste Special* dialog box you select *Paste link* and Microsoft Word Document Object. Select the *Display as icon* check box and click **OK**.
D.	Copy the information that you need from the source file. Return to your PowerPoint presentation slide and choose **Edit | Paste**. In the *Paste* dialog box you select *Paste* and Microsoft Word Document Object. Select the *Display as icon* check box and click **OK**.

Q2	True or false – if you update the source file an embedded database, the embedded information in the presentation doesn't change.
A.	True.
B.	False.

Q4	To change the source file you ...
A.	Choose **Insert	Object**. In the *Links* dialog box you select the information type you want to change and click the **Open Source** button. Select the file you need and click the **Change Source** button. Click the **Close** button to return to your presentation.
B.	Choose **Edit	Links**. In the *Links* dialog box you select the information type you want to change and click the **Change Source** button. Select the file you need and click the **Open Source** button. Click the **Close** button to return to your presentation.
C.	Choose **Insert	Object**. In the *Links* dialog box you select the information type you want to change and click the **Change Source** button. Select the file you need and click the **Open Source** button. Click the **Close** button to return to your presentation.
D.	Choose **Edit	Links**. In the *Links* dialog box you select the information type you want to change and click the **Change Source** button. Select the file you need and click the **Update Now** button. Click the **Close** button to return to your presentation.

Answers

1: B, **2:** C, **3:** A, **4:** D.

12 *Macros and set-ups*

If you have a large number of slides, and you want to change certain details in some of them – use a different font for certain words, use a special animated effect, or add sound, for example – it can take quite a bit of effort and time to make the changes. Each change involves many steps, but the steps involved in each change are the same. Help is at hand, however! PowerPoint enables you to create macros that automate such repetitive tasks, and enable you to execute all the steps with a single mouse-click. You'll learn how to create and run macros in this chapter.

If you want to present one or other of your custom shows, or publish the presentation on the Internet or your company's intranet, or if the presentation is to run unattended in a kiosk or at a trade show, or if you need to pass the PowerPoint file to someone else, you need to set up your presentation to prepare it for final viewing. And if you want to use slides as graphics in word processed documents or web pages, you need to save the relevant slides as graphics. This chapter shows you how.

New skills

At the end of this chapter you should be able to:

- Record a macro

- Run a macro

- Create a custom button for a macro

- Check macro security levels

- Publish a slide show to the web

- Export slides as graphics

- Confirm slide show settings (custom shows and full shows)

At the end of this chapter you should be able to explain the following terms:

- Macro
- Custom button
- Publishing to the web

This chapter covers the following syllabus points:

- AM 6.2.2.1
- AM 6.3.1.6
- AM 6.6.1.4
- AM 6.6.1.5
- AM 6.8.1.1
- AM 6.8.1.2
- AM 6.8.1.3

Recording macros

A macro is a recorded sequence of actions that can be played back with a single command. Typically, you go through the steps involved in executing a particular task, recording these as a macro. Then, any time you want to execute the same task, you can repeat the entire sequence of steps by choosing a single command or clicking a single button.

Recording a macro is just like taping a piece of music. You press **Record**, go through the sequence of actions you want to include in the macro, then press **Stop**. In the following exercise, you will record a macro that hides the selected text element when the mouse is next clicked.

Exercise 12.1: Recording a macro

Note: To do this exercise, the file EX12.1.PPT must be on your hard disk, as the macro is saved to the same location as the presentation. If you have not already done so, copy EX12.1.PPT from the supplied CD to your computer before starting.

1) Open EX12.1.PPT.

2) Go to slide 21, 'Growth Area: Supermarkets'.

3) Choose **Tools | Macro | Record New Macro**.

4) In the *Record Macro* dialog box, give your macro a name, say where it is to be stored, and give a short description, as below.

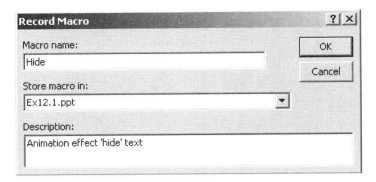

5) Press **OK**. The *Stop Recording* toolbar appears.

You are now in record mode – everything you do between now and pressing the **Stop Recording** button will be included in your macro.

6) Carry out the sequence of tasks that you want to record:

   ■ Choose Slide Show | Custom Animation.

   ■ In the *Custom Animation* dialog box, select the *Text 2* check box.

   ■ In the Effects tab, select *Hide on Next Mouse Click* from the *After animation* drop-down list.

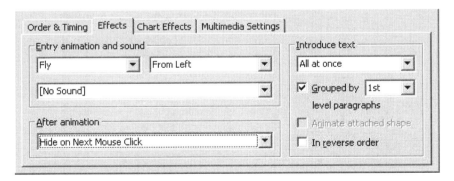

Click **OK**.

7) Press **Stop Recording** on the *Stop Recording* toolbar.

Well done! You've just recorded your first PowerPoint macro.

Macro names and locations

Macro names are best kept short and memorable: short, because you may want to use them on a toolbar button (see below); memorable, because if you have a number of macros, you will find it difficult to remember which is which if they are called names like 'macro1' and 'macro2'.

There are a few rules about naming macros:

- The first character must be a letter.

- The name may be made up of letters, numbers and the underscore character – no spaces or punctuation marks are allowed.

- Certain words are not allowed as macro names, such as Private, Public, Integer and Sub.

But don't worry! If you choose an invalid name, PowerPoint will tell you that it is invalid, and you can choose a different name.

Normally, macros are stored with the presentation for which they are created (as in the exercise above). Alternatively, you can store the macro with the template, so that it can be used with all presentations created from that template.

Running macros

Once you have recorded a macro, you can play it back any time you want to repeat the sequence of actions recorded in the macro. See how simple this is in the next exercise.

Exercise 12.2: Running a macro

1) Open EX12.2.PPT. (If necessary, confirm that you want to **Enable Macros**.)

2) Go to slide 20, 'Growth Area: Farmer Markets'. View it in Slide Show view; then return to Normal view.

3) Select the text that you want to apply the macro to, as below.

4) Choose **Tools | Macro | Macros**.

5) In the *Macro* dialog box, select the *Hide* macro and click the
   Run button.

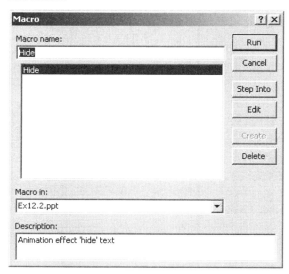

6) In Slide Show view, open slide 20, and note that the animation effect
   has been applied to the slide.

Note: If at any time you want to stop a macro, simply press
CTRL+Break.

Creating custom buttons for macros

You can reduce the effort required to run a macro even further,
by adding a custom button for the macro to a toolbar. In the
next exercise you will create a custom button for the Hide
macro and place it on a PowerPoint toolbar.

Exercise 12.3: Creating a custom button for a macro

1) Open EX12.3.PPT. (If necessary, confirm that you want to **Enable
   Macros**.)

2) Choose **Tools | Customize**.

3) In the *Customize* dialog box click the **Commands** tab and select the
   Macro option.

   Here you see the name of the macro you previously created: 'Hide'.

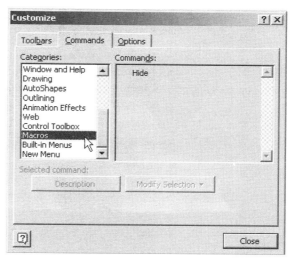

4) Select the 'Hide' macro and drag it to the *Formatting* toolbar.

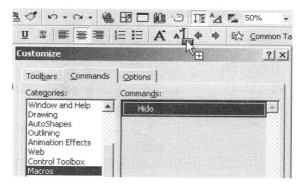

Well done! Your custom button should now look as shown.

Clicking the button will have the same effect as choosing **Tools | Macro | Macros**, selecting the macro, and clicking **Run**.

Macro security

One of the most common ways of transmitting computer viruses is through macros. For this reason, you should be very cautious about opening any file that you receive from someone you don't know, and particularly careful if you know that the file in question contains a macro.

PowerPoint allows you to choose the level of security that applies to presentations that you open: low, medium and high.

- *Low* security level is not generally recommended – all macros are automatically enabled, irrespective of their origin.

- With a *medium* security level, PowerPoint will warn you that a presentation you are opening includes macros, and ask whether or not you want those macros enabled. For instance, if you close a presentation with macros and then open it again, this is what you see on your screen:

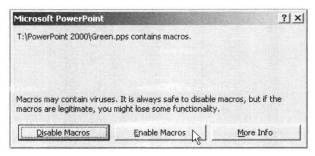

Since you know that the macro in question is harmless, you are safe to click **Enable Macros**. However, if you are unsure, it is better to click **Disable Macros**.

- With a *high* security level, all macros are disabled, with the exception of signed macros coming from trusted sources.

To check your current macro security level, or to change it, choose **Tools | Macro | Security**. In the *Security* dialog box, in the **Security Level** tab, you can see the different security options, one of which is selected. You change the security level by selecting one of the other options. For this presentation, choose the *Medium* option.

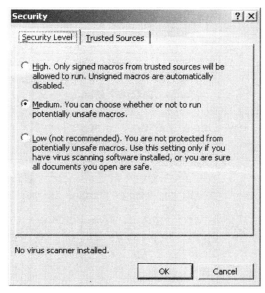

Deleting macros

You will very often use a macro when you are creating your presentation, but have no further use for it after that. It is good practice to delete such a macro, so that people to whom you give copies of the presentation do not have the macro on their PCs.

To delete a macro, follow the steps outlined in the following exercise.

Exercise 12.4: Deleting a macro

1) Open EX12.4.PPT. (If necessary, confirm that you want to **Enable Macros**.)

2) Choose **Tools | Macro | Macros**.

3) Select the macro that you want to delete in the *Macro* dialog box. In your case, it is the 'Hide' macro.

4) Click the **Delete** button.

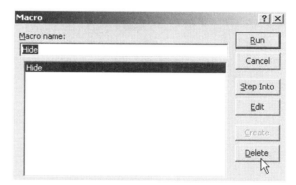

5) PowerPoint asks you to confirm that you want to delete the macro. Click the **Yes** button.

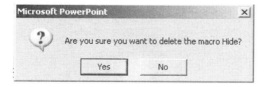

Setting up

You've designed and structured your presentation, set up all the slides, inserted graphics, applied animation and transition effects, rehearsed the timings and recorded your macros. Do you need to do anything else? Well, maybe, depending on how you are going to deliver your presentation.

If you are going to deliver your entire presentation yourself to a live audience, if nobody else is going to use it, either to prepare a similar slide show or to support their own presentation, and if you are sure that you won't have to send the file to someone who might or might not have PowerPoint on their computer, then you don't have to do anything else.

If, however, you want to present one or other of your custom shows, or publish the presentation on the Internet or your company's intranet, or if the presentation is to run unattended in a kiosk or at a trade show, or if you need to pass the PowerPoint file to someone else, you need to set up your presentation to prepare it for final viewing.

Publishing presentations to the web

You can set up your presentation in such a way that it can be viewed with a web browser, either on the Internet or on a corporate intranet. This is called publishing to the web. Your presentation will take on the attributes of a website, such as a navigation bar and an address bar.

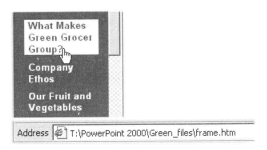

Slide titles will be displayed in a navigation bar, and viewers can simply click on a slide title to access that slide. You can choose to use your presentation animation or not.

The following exercise shows how to publish a presentation to the web.

Exercise 12.5: Publishing a presentation to the web

1) Open EX12.5.PPT.

2) Choose **File | Save As**.

3) In the Save As dialog box, click the arrow to the right of the *Save as type* box. Select the *Web Page (*htm; *.html)* option.

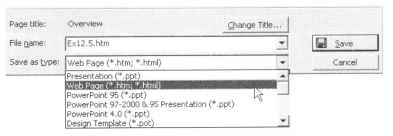

4) Select the location where you want the presentation saved and click the **Publish** button.

5) In the *Publish as Web Page* dialog box, select the *Complete presentation* option in the *Publish what?* section.

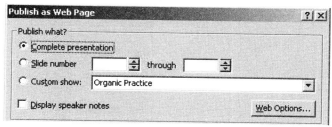

6) Click the **Web Options** button in the *Publish what?* section.

Under the **General** tab, select the options shown below.

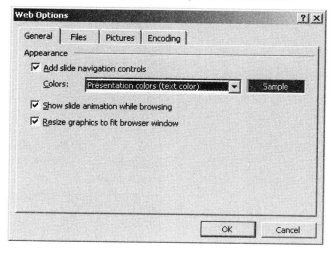

Click **OK**.

7) In the *Browser support* section, select the browser option of your choice. In this case select *Microsoft Internet Explorer 4.0 or later*.

8) In the *Publish a copy as* section, confirm or change the page title and file name. Select the *Open published Web page in browser* check box – this will enable you to see the result of the exercise immediately.

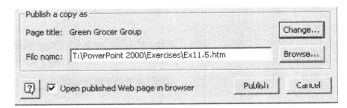

9) Click the **Publish** button.

Your presentation now appears in your Internet browser, with the slide titles in the navigation bar to the left.

You can move from slide to slide sequentially by clicking anywhere in the slide area, or go directly to any slide by clicking on its title in the navigation bar.

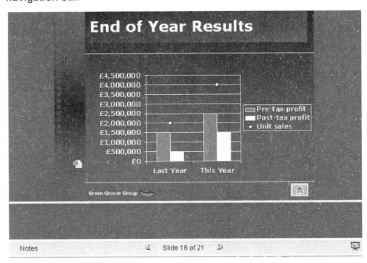

Saving slides as graphics   You can save an individual slide or your entire slide show as graphics that can subsequently be incorporated into a word processed document, for example, or a web page. You might do this if you don't want to publish your slide show on the web in the form of a presentation, but instead want to incorporate some or all of the slides into web pages, as graphic images. In this case, you save your slides in .JPG format. (The different types of graphic files were discussed in Chapter 10.) The following exercise shows you how to save slides as graphics.

Exercise 12.6: Saving slides in JPG format

1) Open EX12.6.PPT.

2) Choose **File | Save As**.

3) In the *Save As* dialog box, click the arrow to the right of the *Save as type* box. Choose the file type you want. You can choose from a range of graphic file formats, including .BMP, .GIF and .JPG. In this case, select the .jpg option (*JPEG File Interchange Format*).

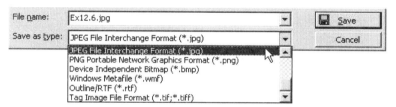

4) Select the location where you want the graphic files saved.

5) Press **Save**.

6) PowerPoint asks you if you want to export all the slides as graphics or just the current slide. Click **Yes**, as you want to create a graphic file for each slide in the presentation.

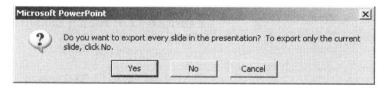

7) PowerPoint tells you that each slide has been saved in a sub-folder of the location you specified. (Here the sub-folder is called Ex12.6.) Click **OK**.

The graphic files are named SLIDE1.JPG, SLIDE2.JPG, etc. They can now be included in web pages, inserted into Word documents, or edited in a graphics application. Note that if you do make them available on a website, they will act as ordinary graphics – they will not have any of the navigation features of an interactive presentation.

Setting up for a live audience

You can set up your presentation to show one or other of your custom shows, to use manual or automatic timings, to show or not show animations, and to show or not to show the background graphics from the Slide Master.

Hiding background graphics

If you do not want to show the background graphics included in the Slide Master, follow the steps in the exercise below.

Exercise 12.7: Hiding background graphics on one or all slides

1) Open EX12.7.PPT.

2) Choose **Format | Background**.

3) In the *Background* dialog box, select the *Omit background graphics from master* check box.

4) Click the **Apply** button – this means that background graphics will be hidden on the selected slide only. If you want to hide the background graphics for every slide in the presentation, you click **Apply to All**.

5) View the effect of your changes in Slide Show view.

Setting up custom shows

In the following exercise you will set up a custom show for slide show viewing. You will advance the slides manually, and turn off the animation effects.

Exercise 12.8: Setting up a custom show

1) Open EX12.8.PPT.

2) Choose **Slide Show | Set Up Show**.

3) In the *Set Up Show* dialog box, select *Custom show*. Click the arrow to the right of the *Custom show* box and select *Organic Practice* from the list displayed.

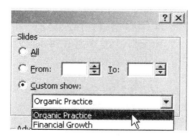

4) Select *Manually* from the *Advance slides* section.

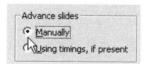

5) Select the following *Show type* options:

- *Presented by speaker (full screen)*.

- *Loop continuously until 'Esc'*.

- *Show without animation*.

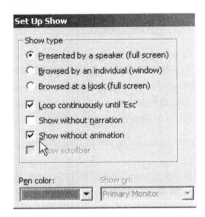

6) Click **OK**.

   Well done! That's your slide show set up to show the Organic Practice custom show, to appear without animation, and to return to the first slide when the last has been seen.

Setting up full shows

The following exercise shows you how to set up a full show, complete with timings and animation, so that it can be opened directly from the desktop, and used by someone who does not have PowerPoint on their PC. This show will also loop continuously, so that it is suitable for unattended use at a trade exhibition, for example.

Exercise 12.9: Setting up a full show

1) Open EX12.9.PPT.

2) Choose **Slide Show | Set Up Show**.

3) In the *Set Up Show* dialog box, select the following *Show type* options:

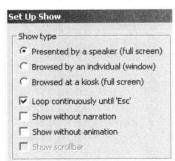

4) Select the following *Slides* options:

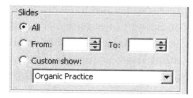

5) Select the following *Advance slides* option:

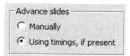

6) Click the **OK** button.

7) Choose **File | Save As**. Click the arrow to the right of the *Save as type* box and choose *PowerPoint Show (*.pps)*

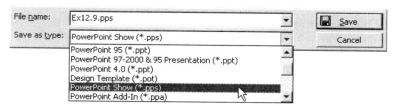

Click **OK**.

To deactivate continuous looping, choose **Slide Show | Set Up Show** and deselect the *Loop continuously until 'Esc'* check box.

You've now done *everything* you need for a successful PowerPoint presentation, and finished the ECDL Advanced Presentation course. Well done!

Chapter 12: summary   A *macro* is a recorded sequence of actions that can be played back with a single command. Recording and running macros is similar to recording and playing back a piece of music. You can create a *custom* button for a macro. If you decide that you no longer need the macro, you can *delete* it from your PowerPoint presentation.

When you are satisfied with the content of your presentation, you can set it up for final viewing. Your set-up will depend on the conditions under which the presentation will be used – live, in support of a speaker; viewed on a website; unattended at a trade show; or attached to an e-mail. You can *publish your presentation to the web*, in which case the presentation will be navigable in a web browser in the same way as in PowerPoint.

You can also export one or all *slides as graphics* (.JPGs) that can be incorporated as static images in web pages or word processing documents. You can exercise a variety of options when setting up your show: hide the background graphics, run a custom show or remove the animation. These options are available from the **Set Up Show** menu.

Chapter 12: quick quiz

Circle the correct answer to each of the following multiple-choice questions about macros and set-ups.

Q1	Which of the following is a valid macro name?
A.	2004macro.
B.	2004 macro.
C.	2004_macro.
D.	macro_2004.

Q2	How do you create a custom button for a macro?
A.	Choose **Tools	Customize**. Under the **Toolbars** tab select the *Macro* option. Select the macro you have created and drag it to the toolbar.
B.	Choose **Tools	Options**. Under the **Commands** tab select the *Macro* option. Select the macro you have created and drag it to the toolbar.
C.	Choose **Tools	Customize**. Under the **Commands** tab select the *Macro* option. Select the macro you have created and drag it to the toolbar.
D.	Choose **Tools	Customize**. Under the **Options** tab select the *Macro* option. Select the macro you have created and drag it to the toolbar.

Q3	True or false – slides saved as jpeg cannot be edited in the Internet browser.
A.	False.
B.	True.

Q4	How do you set up a show to run without animation?
A.	Choose **Slide Show	Set Up Show**, under the *Slides* section select the *Show without animation* check box and click **OK**.
B.	Choose **Slide Show	Custom Shows**, under the *Show type* section select the *Show without animation* check box and click **OK**.
C.	Choose **Slide Show	Set Up Show**, under the *Show type* section select the *Show without animation* check box and click **OK**.
D.	Choose **Slide Show	Set Up Show**, under the *Show type* section select the *Show without narration* check box and click **OK**.

Answers

1: D, **2**: C, **3**: B, **4**: C.

Index

Licensing Agreement

This book comes with a CD software package. By opening this package, you are agreeing to be bound by the following:

The software contained on this CD is, in many cases, copyrighted, and all rights are reserved by the individual licensing agreements associated with each piece of software contained on the CD. THIS SOFTWARE IS PROVIDED FREE OF CHARGE, AS IS, AND WITHOUT WARRANTY OF ANY KIND, EITHER EXPRESSED OR IMPLIED, INCLUDING, BUT NOT LIMITED TO, THE IMPLIED WARRANTIES OF MERCHANTABILITY AND FITNESS FOR A PARTICULAR PURPOSE. Neither the book publisher nor its dealers and its distributors assumes any liability for any alleged or actual damages arising for the use of this software.